# LETTERS
*from*
# VIETNAM

# LETTERS

## *from*

# VIETNAM

*Edited by*

## BILL ADLER

PRESIDIO
PRESS

BALLANTINE BOOKS • NEW YORK

A Presidio Press Book

Published by The Random House Publishing Group
Copyright © 2003 by Bill Adler

All rights reserved under International and Pan-American Copyright
Conventions. Published in the United States by The Random House Publishing
Group, a division of Random House, Inc., New York, and simultaneously
in Canada by Random House of Canada Limited, Toronto.

Presidio Press and colophon are trademarks of Random House, Inc.

www.presidiopress.com

The Cataloging-in-Publication data is available
from the Library of Congress

ISBN 0-8914-1831-8

Book design by Holly Johnson

Manufactured in the United States of America

First Edition: November 2003

1 3 5 7 9 10 8 6 4 2

# CONTENTS

# INTRODUCTION

The compelling emotions and perceptions experienced by soldiers in battle contain a universal timelessness that transcends the historical eras, technologies, and cultures in which wars are fought. The mosaic of firsthand descriptions, reflections, and raw emotions contained in this new edition of *Letters from Vietnam* went into production while the world was watching American soldiers and Marines engaged in the battle for Baghdad. Vietnam was considered the first "television war," but the Second Gulf War became the first "reality TV" battle zone, where viewers followed individual military companies day-to-day with "embedded" cameras and broadcast reporters. Although stunningly hypnotic to an audience, graphic images of combat do not adequately convey the inner feelings of those whose lives are on the line moment to moment. It is candid letters, such as those contained in this book, written by warriors to their loved ones, that provide us with the most intimate reality of their experience.

This book of letters, which the veterans or their families have chosen to share, is a collective personal history of the period of conventional combat in Vietnam from the period when President Lyndon Johnson escalated the conflict in 1965 until the closing days of the U.S. involvement in 1972–73. Those who came of age during that era may remember that returning soldiers, abandoned by the politicians who sent them to Southeast Asia as part of the moral crusade of the Cold War, were vilified by much of the popular media and intelligensia. The only real support and sanctuary they found was in the love of family and close friends who anxiously awaited their return. The frankness of the letters in this book embodies that bond of trust. A new generation of readers, detached from the political emotions of the Vietnam era, may be more receptive to the soldiers' accounts of the uncertainty of combat. The letters describe blinding jungles, searing 125 degree tropical heat, the snakes, the insects of all kinds, the dust, the monsoon rain, ankle-deep mud, the malaria pills, the spiders. They chafe at the debilitating "rules of engagement" imposed by politicians far away from the war zone who gave the advantage to ruthlessly tenacious Vietnamese communist fighters. The guerrilla disguised in civilian clothes employed nightmarish tactics, such as using women and children as saboteurs, hindering American troops who did not have the advantages of today's high-tech military or the luxury of an objective mass media.

The letter writers include infantry soldiers and Marines, helicopter pilots, medical aid workers and Red Cross "Donut Dollies"—young women who did not participate in combat but were "morale boosters" near the front lines who shared the emotions, hopes, and dreams of the American fighting men. Like epic poetry written in blood from the young warriors' hearts, we get a more accurate perceptual portrait of war than a lurid photograph or film clip could possibly convey. From page to page, we absorb the loneliness that a soldier must endure as he stares into the face of death, the comradery and unselfishness among fellow warriors who share a fragile sense of mortality, and the duty and honor in which they represent their country, regardless of the unfaithfulness of national leaders who sent them into harm's way.

In one of many haunting passages in this book of letters, a young father, James Kline, member of the U.S. Navy, writes from

Da Nang, Vietnam, to his only child, seven-year-old Ricky, on the burdens and responsibilities of being a soldier and a father.

> Give your Mother a big hug and kiss for me and remember you are the man of the house while I am away. . . . There are a lot of fathers here that are making their sacrifice so that their sons and you may have a free country to grow up in—you have the right to worship as you choose and to make of yourself as you see fit. These are only simple things to you and me. But there are very few in this world who have this right . . . Remember me and all the others over here in your prayers and ask Him [God] to help people see the folly of all the fighting and bickering that goes on in this troubled world. Above all I want you to know that I'm proud that I have a chance to do my part to make all of these things available to you.

The rock-solid values expressed by James Kline and other warriors found in this book epitomize the motivation that has guided American citizen-soldiers from the time of George Washington through today's conflict against international terrorism. The enduring wisdom expressed in these letters, forged in the inferno of the Vietnam War, should never be forgotten.

—Al Santoli, author of *New York Times* best-seller
*Everything We Had: An Oral History of the Vietnam War*
Washington, D.C.
April 5, 2003

# COMBAT

*"In less than one minute,*
*a relatively peaceful day went straight to hell."*

CORPORAL JON JOHNSON *of Ohio served with the Marine Corps in Delta Company, 1st Battalion, 5th Marine Regiment, 1st Marine Division, while in Vietnam. His honors include the National Defense Service Medal, Vietnamese Service Medal with two stars, and the Presidential Unit Citation.*

*After returning home to Ohio from Vietnam, Corporal Johnson was stationed at Camp Lejeune, North Carolina, and was soon after selected to serve with the Marine security detachment at the Canadian World Exposition in Montreal, Canada, in 1967. Corporal Johnson is active in the Marine Corps League and is the Senior Vice Commander at his Veterans of Foreign Wars chapter.*

*He wrote the following letter home to his parents and wife in Sidney, Ohio.*

*PFC Jon Johnson, at MCAS Kaneohe Bay, Hawaii, before his departure to Vietnam (photographer unknown)*

8 April 1966

Dear Mom & Dad & Peggy,

Operation Jackstay is over. I guess now I'm a veteran. Nothing they could have done would have prepared us for this. We now know the training in Hawaii and the Philippines was a piece of cake. God doesn't know about the Mekong Delta, He didn't create that hellhole. I think when He rested, the devil slipped one in on him. They told us before we went in that we were the first American unit to operate that far south in the war. I think everyone else had more brains. Maybe when I'm out of the Marines I'll be proud of this, I'm just too tired to feel anything.

We lost some good guys. How do you explain this in a letter? One minute they were there, then dead. I have no idea why I'm still here. Our third night into the operation we set up on the high ground, what there was of it, and all of a sudden I heard a shell coming in. It was the most horrifying sound I could imagine. I was in position with another guy, George from Boston, and it was as dark as it could be. I can't describe that sound. It would be close if I said it sounded like a freight train coming out of the sky. No warning, just that sound. My instincts told me that it was up and to my left. Just as I looked that way it hit about 100 feet from me. The flash of light and explosion was tremendous. It knocked me stupid. Next thing I knew I was laying on my back wondering why the voices were so far away, and my head felt like there was a basketball inside trying to get out. For some reason George kept asking me if I was dead, and I thought why the hell didn't he shut up. Finally things started coming back into focus and I heard the screams. I told George to get ready because I thought there was going to be an attack soon. Then I noticed I was on his right. I was on his left before the shell hit. Sgt. Joyce comes running by and asked for help with the wounded. All we could do was crawl around in the darkness feeling for bodies. I found the foot of someone and told him. He had a red lens flashlight and turned it on. It was Sgt. Herrera, dead. I went back to my position, and the corpsman was working on George. He had been hit in the leg with shrapnel but would remain with us. The shell killed two and wounded nine. That was it, just one shell. But my God what a price.

We're on our way back to Subic Bay now to pick up replacements and take on supplies. The whole atmosphere has changed. No more chicken shit stuff. After Subic we're going on another operation. They say this one is near the DMZ. It has to be better than the Mekong Delta.

Sorry to be so down in the dumps. I'm just tired, very tired. Don't expect many letters because we have no idea when we will return to Vietnam. I don't take writing gear with me on an operation. Wouldn't have time to write anyway.

I'm supposed to feel something for those we lost. Wish to God I knew what.

Love You Mom—Love You Dad.

I love you Peggy.

Your son & husband,

Jon

MARINE JOE PAIS *described his reactions to the war in a letter to his mother in Raton, New Mexico.*

August 30, 1965

Dear Mom,

. . . Mom, I know I will never be the same Joe. Last night I lost one of my best buddies. It wasn't Bob, but he used to run around with us. Somehow the VC got through our lines and threw a grenade into where my buddy was sleeping. One of my other buddies was wounded seriously and he's expected to die any time. You know, Mom, things didn't really bother me until we got out here in the bad part of Da Nang. And now I lose two of my buddies. It's hard, Mom, to get over something like this, that's why I say it's gonna be different.

I can't even smile anymore, nothing seems funny to me, everything is serious now. Once I get out of here I never want to hear another word about Vietnam or wars. You read in the papers about demonstrators and all this other bull . . . they ask why we are over here. Well we're stopping communism over here instead of in the people's backyard back home in the USA. And we're doing a damn good job over here and we'll keep on doing a good job. Our Marine Corps saying is "Death Before Dishonor."

Well the rainy season has finally moved in. It rains just about every day now. Sometimes all day and all night.

I've moved to a new position now, I'm squad leader. I'm in charge of six men. Of course I'm still in heavy machine guns, our job is real dangerous, our life expectancy in combat is seven seconds. I'll be home though, I won't let anything stop me.

I sure would like to see my family, especially my little niece. It's gonna be like a new world when I get home. Everything is gonna be so different. You know I haven't slept in a good old bed since Jan. 2. Out here we sleep on a shelter half or a poncho with one blanket. The hard ground doesn't even bother me anymore. Hot chow, we very seldom get that. We've been eating C-rations ever since we got here. I'm gonna have a straight back and an iron stomach. No more food poison for me. It wouldn't even bother me. . . .

Well, Mom, I'm gonna have to rush off now. I'll write more later. God bless you.

I love you,

Joe

SERGEANT F. LEE HUDSON III *of New Jersey served with the U.S. Army Radio Teletype Section Chief 6th/15th Field Artillery, 1st Infantry Division and 1st/7th Field Artillery, 1st Infantry Division. He arrived at Vung Tau, Vietnam, from USNS* Gordon *on June 1967 and left Vietnam on April 24, 1968. He assisted the field artillery in many engagements, including the Tet Offensive. He was awarded the Army Commendation Medal.*

*Sergeant Hudson wrote the following letter home to his parents, Fred and Edith Hudson, of Pine Hill, New Jersey.*

*Sergeant F. Lee Hudson III in the lookout tower on the Di An perimeter (photographer unknown)*

2 Feb. 68

Dear Mom and Dad,

I keep writing these letters every day just to let you know that I'm all right. This is another letter written with a flashlight. I know you must be pretty worried with all the action that is going on. The only thing I'm worried about is what I heard on the radio today. Johnson is thinking about extending all enlisted men who are in the Army. I'd hate to spend more than two years in the Army.

Today has really been a wild one. Just before noon today everybody was rushed over to the ammo dump. Because of all the firing in the last few days, our batteries are running low on ammunition. So today a rush convoy from Long Binh came up with the ammo and the guys had to break it down and restack it for helicopters. They worked right through lunch and dinner. Now it's eight o'clock and they're still working.

The ammo pickup area is right near our perimeter, and around six o'clock we had incoming small arms fire from Charlie. The whole base is under alert, but after the firing stopped they went back to work again. We're still under alert and this may be on for a few more days. We haven't been able to get any laundry in or out and most of us are wearing dirty clothes. Today we got a little mail. Little incidents have been occurring all over the area and Charlie seems to be everywhere. Well now I've got to get back to work. I'll write again tomorrow. Take care and don't worry.

Love,

Lee

CHIEF WARRANT OFFICER ANTHONY B. DE ANGELIS *served with the U.S. Army during his tour of duty in Vietnam from February 1967 to January 1968, departing the day of the Tet Offensive. He was awarded the Bronze Service Medal for Meritorious Service and the Vietnam Service Medal with two battle stars.*

*He sent the following letter to Lis C. De Angelis, his wife, to assure her that he was fine since he was involved in a major attack that was in the news at the time in June 1967.*

*Chief Warrant Officer Anthony De Angelis*
*(photo by 1st Lt. Mike Sunshine)*

June 10, 1967
Plei-Ku, Vietnam

Dear Darling,

Just in case you already heard about our attack this morning I don't want you to worry. I'm alright. You'll have to excuse this letter as I have had only two hours sleep in the last 26 hours, and my arm still hurts from the tetanus shot I just got. Early this morning, about

14

1:30 A.M., Mr. "B" woke me up and said quite seriously, "O.K., Tony, let's go, this is it." I was still half asleep, but the whooshing staccato of booms signaled my senses as to what he was talking about. Like the precise ass that I am, I faultlessly dressed myself to include lacing and tying my boots, and then ran a quarter of a mile to our defense bunker while the mortars were incoming. En route I ran into some barbed wire which cut me up a little, thus the reason for the tetanus shot. When I got to the bunker, the only ones there were Captain Jefferson (our Negro battery commander), my personnel sergeant, the supply sergeant, and a few privates. It was raining like hell and they had already begun counter mortar fire. The regular mortar crew were pinned down in a bunker near the billets, so there I was pitching in with the others passing mortar ammo to Cpt. Jeff who was lobbing them out. We were firing every 30 seconds, which meant we had to really hustle; and we were! We were firing all kinds of illuminating flares over the area where we seen them coming from, and the firing battery of 105s right next to us was lobbing the shells into the area. We were very fortunate that we suffered no casualties except for scratches and bruises as a result of getting to positions. However, our sister units on the hill here with us were not as lucky. They sustained 41 casualties (all wounded as far as I know). The sky above us was like daylight while we were firing, and a good thing, too, because as fast as the men got hit, the medevac choppers with their red cross on the side were flying right over our position to get the men out, and we had to be careful we didn't hit them with mortars, as fast as we were firing. They had guts to fly through that barrage of both incoming and outgoing garbage. The attack lasted about two hours, but we continued firing the rest of the night to insure against further attack. We didn't get the all clear until eight A.M. this morning and then we went back to work, where I am at now. This was the first time the hill has ever been attacked, so you can guess a lot of people were quite surprised.

Anyhow, everybody acted beautifully and I wouldn't worry about these people not knowing what to do in a similar situation. The new battalion CO was very pleased with the way our battalion reacted.

The Middle East reports are really confusing. I certainly hope it settles down quick. I find it hard to believe Nasser resigned. It appears he had no other choice and was banking on his people to beg him not to. Well, darling, it's been a long night. I'm too tired to write more, but I want to. Darling, I love you very much; Christian and Michael, too. Mr. Caruso called me this morning to see if I was alright. His unit took a lot of casualties. It reminds me, too, that I better call Mike as I know he's aware of our attack and I don't want him to be concerned. Darling, I'm sorry but I don't know how it happened, but I lost the Saint Christopher medal you gave me; it must have come loose from the chain. I feel real bad about it, as anything from you I consider very special. Darling, I love you. Give the boys my love.

Love always,
Tony

FIRST LIEUTENANT JAMES MICHENER *wrote the following letter home to his parents while he was a helicopter pilot in Vietnam from 1966 to 1967. In addition, he served as personal pilot for Major General Byong H. Lew, Commanding General, Republic of Korea Tiger Division, II Corps, Vietnam. His honors include the Air Medal with V device (for valor) and the Bronze Star.*

*Warrant Officer 1 James Michener, 22, 129th Assault Helicopter Company, supporting the 101st Airborne Division, Phan Thiet, Vietnam, March 1967 (photographer unknown)*

17 November 1966
Tuy Hoa, Vietnam

Dear [names omitted],

I'm exhausted and have been away from Tuy Hoa for almost a week. Thus I was unable to write. On my return I found eight letters, two newspapers, and two packages. This was wonderful but now I'll have to spend several evenings trying to catch up on correspondence.

A week ago today my platoon, the 1st Platoon, departed for Dong Tre and was to come home Sunday night—tonight is Thursday. But the time was lengthened until noon Tuesday.

Dong Tre is a Vietnamese village housing a Special Forces camp. We were there to furnish air support to units of the IV (Fourth) Infantry Division ("Ivy Division") and the 101st Airborne Division ("Screaming Eagles"). These units were making a general sweep of an area about one hundred miles square. They were looking for Victor Charlie ("VC")—that's what we call him.

Both units ran into a little action from time to time. But nothing big. Captured 41 North Vietnamese soldiers and killed 56. Plus quite a cache of weapons was found. Enough to think that possibly a battalion-sized unit might have been out there.

Of course we were constantly busy hauling food and supplies to the men in the field. We made several combat assaults also, but the areas proved moderately secure. The weather, especially when visibility was zero-zero, posed a big problem as the region is not flat—it's mountainous.

One of my classmates in the company (the 129th) and a major (also in the 129th) crashed into a mountaintop while trying to land on it—the weather was closing in—but all crew members walked away from the accident. The aircraft was totally destroyed.

As a matter of fact, for every chopper that the "VC" (Viet Cong) shoot down, three go down in accidents not related to hostile fire. So the problem is not the Viet Cong as I look at it. The problem is ourselves. I try to be as safety conscious as I can. I don't want to get killed in an accident.

Our quarters at Dong Tre were poor. But one can't have everything all the time. In the way of accommodations, Dong Tre made what little we have here at Tuy Hoa seem "super."

We had eight ships at Dong Tre for the period we were there. And only two tents to house the crews, four people per chopper. In a way I'm glad the weather wasn't sunny: canvas tents can get terribly hot and hold the heat at night. But the floor was dirt, and with the wretched rain it soon turned to mud.

I tried to shower every night but there was only a well in Dong

Tre. We would lower a metal "ammo" tray attached to a long piece of "commo" wire into the well and haul our water up. Then we would pour it into a basin and have another person pour it over us. And rub like mad with the soap, as a basin of water doesn't go very far. The primitive system worked O.K.; after a long day in the pilot's seat any kind of water for washing will do.

We were furnished with potable water for drinking. And now and then a ship would come in with a case or two of soda and beer. The "101st" cooked breakfast and supper for us. Lunch was always C-rations. And quite often the same for supper, as we seldom got back in time for the last meal of the day no matter where we were. We started flying at dawn and stopped when we couldn't see any longer, the sun having already set.

While we were up there, the ship CWO Figueroa and I were flying took one round from a sniper hidden in a tree line. A 7.62mm round came through the skin of the aircraft just aft of the left chin bubble, proceeded upward through ¼ inch cast aluminum alloy and into the armor plate beneath the pilot's seat (left-hand side). The hole in the aluminum was as big as a quarter.

It was lucky for CWO Figueroa that he wasn't shot in the leg. It was a close call. Too close for comfort. We were flying low level at the time and rounding a bend in a river we were following westward. Steep hills came down on both sides—sort of like a mountain pass. It was an excellent place for Charlie to get off an accurate shot.

We discovered the hole after landing at a "red-leg" (artillery) unit up the river a bit. Later the same day gunships combed the area and took on heavy automatic weapons fire from the hill on the south side of the river. They were able to put rockets, machine-gun fire, and grenades into the hillside. Afterwards, due to poor weather I flew through the pass again; this time it was absolutely quiet.

Yesterday I was on the same river but farther east. On the south side another sniper got off about five bursts of some type of automatic weapon aimed at my ship. But he was a poor shot and missed.

As we approached several tree-lined paddies I saw two people duck under the trees. When we passed over the spot we heard gunfire. But as we were flying low level, we were there and gone so fast—three feet over the treetops at 100 or 110 mph, a thrilling way to move across Vietnamese landscape by anyone's definition of the word "move"—it wasn't likely they'd nail us.

Of course a pass is a different story. Especially if you're at the bottom and Charlie's on the top. But these are the chances everyone takes for granted in Vietnam daily. In the whole history of the 129th to date, only one ship's been lost to hostile action.

I try to be as safe as possible on the ground and in the air. And never take risks that can be avoided. Of course it has to be the mission first, but the pilot always makes the decision to go or not to go. So I'm sure I'll come home—return Stateside—in one piece.

The ground pounder (the infantryman) is the individual I worry about. He takes more risks. And then there are accidents. The second morning I was at Dong Tre two GIs were burning C-ration boxes and it turned out there were two grenades in one box. The troops hadn't inspected the boxes. An hour later CWO Figueroa and I had to fly the body of one of the soldiers back to a medical unit (actually a morgue) here in Tuy Hoa.

That type of thing is ever so sad. I'd hate to be the parents. Just carelessness. The family will never be told the truth because it's not supposed to happen. But such a "blood" price to pay. And not an uncommon tale in Vietnam at all. As fate would have it, the other GI came away with mere flesh wounds.

How odd and unpredictable are individual men's destinies. One dies. One lives. A third observes each and writes about both. How long will the snuffing out of a life live in my memory? The taking of that life for no sensible reason, what will its aftereffect be? Will it change who I am?

Yesterday, while WO Gates and I were flying for the "Fourth," my ship was called on to search a stretch of river—exactly the same place CWO Figueroa and I took that single "hit" several days ago—for a GI who had been swept away by the current. One of the companies was trying to make a river crossing, and this particular soldier volunteered, I guess, to give it a try. Well, it rained hard the night before last and throughout yesterday morning. During his attempt yesterday afternoon, the current pulled the GI under. I imagine he was carrying a full pack.

We never did find him. We flew as slow as we dared up and down the raging river several times near where the top sergeant said the trouble had begun. Of course the streams leading into the river itself were swollen. Probably he'll never be found. But if the ground commander had thought twice he might have tied a rope to the soldier beforehand and prevented the tragedy.

Individual fate seems relatively minor when compared to the Big Picture. But losing a life is still a tremendous loss. Of course you'll never hear stories like these in the states because they're hushed up for the parents' sake if nothing else. I guess it stands to reason. But such incidents are all too common.

By the way, the company that got stranded by the river, WO Gates and I, with our lone ship, moved the entire unit to safe ground in an hour. Ninety some troops. But enough "war stories" for one night. As you can see, however, the view is somewhat different from this side of the Pacific.

Yesterday I flew 10 hours and 10 minutes, "10 + 10." That's two days worth of flying by U.S. Army Aviation standards. Our company was involved all day today airlifting a battalion. It took us seven hours and 35 minutes, "7 + 35." All formation flying. That's why I'm so tired. Sure would be nice to have a day off. It's been about two weeks since I've had any time but evenings to myself.

I've got a sandbag floor in the tent now. Makes it much nicer. But guess I mentioned improvements before . . .

. . . To all of you, I don't know if it seems like I've been gone very long or not. Of course time flies by here. Hope I can say that throughout my tour.

The Air Force is moving in just north of us. It took over a small Army airfield. Built a runway 10,000 feet (that's two miles!) long. One fighter squadron consisting of 18 F-4C jets is already based there. Another squadron is due soon. Things could become a bit hairy for us chopper drivers with so much jet traffic cruising around Tuy Hoa.

But there are the new airfield's good points: a complete instrument landing and departure system. That could come in handy if I get caught sometime in bad weather and have to fly to Tuy Hoa by instruments alone. I could find home and land *in one piece.* . . .

Love,

Jimmy

SERGEANT GEORGE R. BASSETT *of Portland, Maine, served in the U.S. Army in Vietnam. He arrived in Vietnam in July 1965 aboard the troop carrier USS Leroy Eltinge as part of a fire brigade. He returned to the U.S. in June 1966 after serving a year tour as an Automatic Rifleman with the 1st Brigade, 101st Airborne Division V.N. Ten months later he voluntarily returned to Vietnam to complete a second tour of duty as a machine gunner on a helicopter. His honors include the Purple Heart and a Citation for Bravery Under Fire.*

*Sergeant Bassett wrote the following letter home to his parents, Veronica and George E. Bassett, in Limestone, Maine, detailing operations against hostile forces by Company B, 2/502 Abn. Inf., 101st Airborne Brigade (detached) in the mountainous jungles of Tuy Hoa Province, Republic of Vietnam, against the 95th People's Army, North Vietnam.*

30 July 67

Dear Dad, Mom + Kids;

I hope this finds you all in the best of health and spirits, also all settled in your new home.

Well, I finally made it and am all squared away in my new company. We landed at Can Rahn Bay, (as before) then I had to go to Nha Trang for 3 days and finally to my unit.

The heat doesn't seem to bother me much. Maby I got acclimatized in Kentucky. This is the last month of the monsoon season and all is mud here.

I am at Pleiku, which is 23 miles from the cambodian border. Got my machinegunner job on a chopper as I wanted.

*Letter home from Sergeant George R. Bassett, 1967*

Will probably start flying in a couple of days. When we support a unit, we go to the field and stay with them when the situation permits.

I hope your 800 mi trip wasn't too bad for you. Wish I could have been there to help with the driving I immagine everyone finds it kind of hot there except for Dad. Hope you have good personel and working conditions there Dad. Don't want you to get any ulcers. Sure had a good time on leave, especially deep sea fishing.

Well will go now. Expect to hear from you all soon. Love + miss you.

Lots of Love
George

E-5 George R. Bassett,
170th Assault Helicopter Co.
A.P.O. S.F. 96318

25

28 March 66
Tuy Hoa, V.N.

Dear Mom, Dad, and Kids:

I hope that you are all fine and that everything is going well for you. I'm sure some happy for you on your promotion, Dad, as I know that you really worked hard for it and deserve it. Bet you were surprised making it to your 1st time in for it, weren't you?

I haven't got my box yet Mom, but I imagine it is in Tuy Hoa waiting for me. They only bring the mail (letters) to the field as we wouldn't be able to carry the packages with us (we carry about 45 lbs. of equipment on us as it is).

We came out of the jungle last night and have set up camp in the paddies. Our company is in reserve right now due to our low strength. We have had 22 noncombat casualties (malaria, broken bones, etc.) plus a lot of battle casualties. Our colonel talked to us yesterday and told us we were going into reserve and that he was immensely proud of us for spearheading the brigade for the last two months. He only guaranteed us 24 hours rest. Nice guy!

One of the guys in my fire team slipped on a rock and ruptured himself and paralyzed his left leg. We carried him for a day and a half to get him to the rice paddies where a medevac could take him to the hospital. We had to go down this one last valley about 3000 m. long to reach the paddies and we ran into VC. They had been congregating here trying to get away from us as we swept to the south. We got to within 300 m. of the paddies, fighting all the way, when we were finally pinned down on a narrow path flanked by high ridges on both sides. We called in artillery on the VC pinning us down. On the first round, the shrapnel came a little close to us so we called and told them to adjust it. They did so and the next volley (six rounds of 105mm howitzers) landed in the middle of us. My squad. It got five men in back of me and four in front of me. Campbell (on the stretcher) and I were the only ones that didn't get hit and we were in the middle of everybody that did get hit. I heard a man screaming about 20 ft. in back of me. He hollered, "Get it off me, it's burning me." I ran back to the noise but couldn't see anything, as the place was covered with green smoke. The man was blown off the path a little ways down a bank. I started feeling around and got his hand and pulled him a couple of feet up towards the path. He caught on the vegetation and I lost my grip on him. I got a glimpse of his hand through the green smoke and saw he was colored and then I knew who it was. The M-79 Grenade Gunner in my squad. He was still hollering and saying he was hurting. I felt around in the smoke and got hold of his load leaving equip. and pulled him up to the path. This wounded guy was trying to help me but couldn't. He started hollering and beating his head against a rock at something he had seen. When I got him on the path I realized where the smoke was coming from and got rid of it. A smoke grenade (signal) he had on his shoulder harness had been detonated by the artillery. When the smoke cleared, I looked at him. He was still talking. The grenade had burned his back, and the artillery had hit him in the face, chest, and took big hunks out of the upper part of his leg and cut his foot off. That is what the other guy saw that cracked him up. The medics fixed everybody up as best they could. Two died later, guess the rest will be okay. Gun choppers were called in to give up supporting fire while we carried the wounded past the snipers to the paddies (it was almost dark now). We started down two hours after the artillery got us. I was helping carry a poncho litter, and one of the machine gunners in a chopper opened up on us by mistake. He wounded a man in the 3rd platoon and a ricochet hit me in the leg. About ½ the copper bullet casing stuck in my leg. The lead spewed out of it when it hit the rock. It was so minor it only required a Band-Aid. I thought I was hit bad before I looked. I sure thanked God a lot that day and often since.

We are succeeding in our mission here. We have beaten the famous 95th PAUN (N.V.) Regiment down to their knees. We learned from prisoners we took when we captured one of their hospitals that the regiment was below 50% strength, and that they were hunting for food because we guarded the harvest and they couldn't get any of it.

Westmoreland wants us to annihilate them or make the rest of the regiment surrender. Neither fate has ever been inflicted on a complete NVA regiment before.

We hold the best average in V.N. for captured weapons to dead gooks. One weapon for each three gooks. The Marines are second with one to 16.

Don't worry about me carrying any VC patches, Dad. This war isn't by the Geneva Convention. Charlie doesn't take any prisoners nor do we. Only when the CO sees them first. We shoot the wounded. We only keep a prisoner if there is an LZ (landing zone) near where a chopper can come in and get him out. Charlie has no facilities for keeping prisoners nor any use for them.

Therefore surrender is not even considered in a hopeless situation. He has only got about five men from our brigade. We found two of them that had their privates in their mouth, sewn shut, hanging by their ankles from a tree.

That's when they gave us hatchets and we lifted a couple heads. Also tied bodies on the fenders of 2 ½ ton trucks and drove through the village as a warning. We haven't had any mutilations since then that we know about.

Guess I told you they took our hatchets away.

Did you see my buddy on "I've got a secret" with the hole in his helmet? This is his picture. He is also in some of my slides. Haven't gotten money from telegram yet. Please drop line to return to you at Bank of America in Bangkok.

Well, time to go I guess. Generally speaking I guess I'm fine but a little shaky. Am really looking forward to getting home. Tell Grand got a letter will answer as soon as possible. They sure are nice folks.

All my love,
Georgie

*These letters, written by* MARINE SERGEANT GEORGE CARVER *to his sister in Brooklyn, New York, convey some of the pressures and strains imposed upon a soldier during extended periods of battle.*

22 Sept. 1965

Dear Barbara,

. . . I'm sorry that I've neglected to write, but I've been so tired and tensed up that I hardly know what I'm doing at times. It has gotten to the point where I'm still groggy and half alert an hour and a half after I've been up. I wish I knew when they were going to give us some time off. It had better be soon, as most of us have been working 18 and 20 hours a day, besides having 12 hours of guard every fourth night. . . .

Was in VC territory this morning and had a couple of shots go whizzing past our vehicle. I wish these little SOBs would come out in the open so we could "clean their clocks" for them. We have a "code of ethics" over here. Don't shoot at them unless they shoot at you first. Just great, isn't it! I sometimes wonder who we are trying to impress over here. . . .

16 Jan. 66

Dear Barbara,

It is now approaching 10 P.M. and the "finale" of our recent "sweep." We are dirty, muddy, wet, and a bit discouraged. The rains have left us but the heat is overwhelming. After so many months of rain, we have forgotten the extreme change of climate.

I sit writing to you with a four-day growth of beard and smelling worse than a pig. Tomorrow we "secure" for a "rest."

Another day is past and a few more of my friends have given their lives for freedom.

There has been considerable talk of peace in the past few days. I guess the U.S. will succumb to the "soft touch" once again.

I don't think the people of the U.S. (including the government) realize the effort and sacrifice we are giving. Have they forgotten the years of 1941–1945 and 1951–1953? These dates are history, as are 1775, 1812, and 1914!

I think not of myself or the ones I have, but for the people of the U.S. and the generations to come.

You may think that this is very silly or stupid, but stop and give a little thought. Are we giving our lives for a stalemate or for victory? Many times I have asked myself this question, and have yet to reach a suitable answer. Maybe I will never know the answer, but I shall continue to the end.

I must close for now, as it is time to move on. Each twig that is broken or the stillness of the animals means that danger may be near. Five months have passed and I'm a "bundle of nerves" and I jump at the littlest thing. . . .

I must close for now, as it is time to "acquire" a few more "feet or yards" for the "glory of Vietnam."

Your loving brother,

George

SERGEANT RON ASHER *wrote the following letters home to his mother, Dorothy Asher. He wrote the first letter just prior to the Tet Offensive from the outpost on the DMZ. He served with the 1st Battalion, 3rd Marines, from February 1967 to March 1968 and, as a member of the Fleet Marine Force, Special Landing Force—Alpha, served in more major operations than any other combat unit. Sergeant Asher received the Presidential Unit citation from Hubert Humphrey in November 1967.*

*Sergeant Ron Asher, aboard the U.S.S.Okinawa, 1967
(photo by his Marine buddy Joe Pierce)*

1967
Jan. 20

Folks—

The last couple of days has been another one of those nightmare experiences. Our platoon (2nd) walked right into a company of gooks. And the bad thing about it was it was 0500 & pitch dark. It was a beautiful ambush & we walked right into it. We went to the field with 45 men, & here is our casualty report: three dead, 23

*31*

**3D MARINE DIVISION (REIN), FMF, VIETNAM.**

Jan 20

Folks -

The last couple of days have been another one of those miserable experiences. Our platoon (2nd) walked right into a company of gooks. And the bad thing about it was it was 0500 + pitch dark.

It was a beautiful ambush + we walked right into it. We went to the field with 45 men, + here is our casualty report: 3 dead; 23 wounded; 1 missing. I lost 3 out of my squad! (all were hit, not killed) leaving me short again. And out of the three, two of them were my gunners, so now I'm in the hole for gunners. When one of the gunners got hit I took over the gun, but I'm getting too

*Sergeant Ron Asher's letter*

wounded, one missing. I lost three out of my squad (all were hit, not killed), leaving me short again. And out of the three, two of them were my gunners, so now I'm in the hole for gunners. When one of the gunners got hit I took over the gun, but I'm getting too damn short for this crap. I can't explain or tell about this on paper, it was just incredible. The gooks were so close we were throwing grenades over their heads. We finally called tanks etc. in & at 1500 we weren't pinned down anymore. I'm beat, I've got to get some sleep, I'll write tomorrow.

Jan. 21

I don't believe it—after we finally kicked the gooks' ass with air strikes & arty & they pulled out, now, a day later, they're right back in the same place. It's an estimated company (reinforced). Now I don't know what will happen. We're on standby as a reactionary force (all 20 of us in the plt.). The damn gooks are planning something big. I just pray it is not where I am. It's getting hairy over here now, I just want out. Guess it wouldn't hurt to say a few prayers for the men over here. I'll try and write more tonite, I'm still a little "shaky." Bye for now—take care & God bless.

Love,

Ron

COLONEL JAMES B. LINCOLN *served two tours in Vietnam, from March 1965 to October 1966 and again from November 1971 to November 1972. He served as an advisor to the South Vietnamese Army and company commander of an artillery battery in the 1st Infantry Division, U.S. Army.*

*Colonel James Lincoln and classmates from West Point class of 1960 together in Vietnam, January, 1966. L to R: Lincoln, Bill Hanne, Ken Richardson (photographer unknown)*

1 Aug. 65

### THE STORY OF AN AMBUSH PATROL

About noon on 30 July we received intelligence that two VC platoons were in the District, with four American prisoners, and were planning to move to the north to join up with a larger VC force that also had American POWs. After discussion with the District chief, we jointly decided we would put out two ambush patrols on the two most likely areas where the VC would have to pass to make their movement to the north. My assistant and the team intelligence Sgt. went to the western location, and I went to the east. I decided to try a new weapon the team had just received—an M-60 machine gun. I guess it is a little unusual for a Captain to carry a machine gun on a patrol, but it is too heavy for the small Vietnamese to carry, and I thought it could make a significant contribution to the mission. The patrol consisted of a heavily armed, large squad—16 men. The patrol leader was the District S-2, a Lieutenant, who has a good amount of combat experience. He was a Regional Force Company Commander for one year. He had previously reconnected the ambush site on a daytime training patrol, knowing that sometime we would return on a night ambush patrol. All men but three were armed with automatic weapons, consisting of Thompson submachine guns and a BAR. Also, each man had three hand grenades, although the ability of the Vietnamese soldier is limited to throw the grenade far enough to get out of the blast area! I was the heaviest armed of all. I had eight hand grenades, including fragmentation, WP, and one CS grenade that is used as a last resort if the VC are overrunning the position. I had the M-60 and 300 rounds of ammo. I weighed about 260 lbs! We departed at 1930, with a route that involved about four kilos of easy walking along the canal bank, then about five kilos of difficult walking thru the rice paddy to the ambush site. I noticed the great weight of the MG after about 30 minutes of walking, not that the dead weight bothered me, it is rather awkward to carry with the 100-round box that is attached to the side of the weapon. Once we hit the rice paddy, I realized I may have bit off more than I could chew. The water varied from knee depth to waist, but the muddy bottom was what made the walking difficult. Balance was the main problem, and I had to walk slow for fear of falling down and possibly eliminating the MG for use at the ambush site. On two occasions I stepped in a hole and the water went up to my neck, but I managed to keep the MG reasonably dry. After two hours of walking in the paddy, I would say that if I had not been to Ranger school, I would not have gone any farther. We finally arrived at the canal shown on the sketch. I proceeded to walk down the trail to the site. There were numerous small bridges and fords that had to be crossed, and they caused us some difficulty. Once we arrived at the location chosen, the position for the MG was in an old concrete bridge abutment that is shown on the map. After the patrol leader finished putting out the men into position, he joined me and the radio operator in the bunker. Prior to the patrol, I had convinced my counterpart to arrange a little artillery support, which he had not thought of himself. We had planned concentrations in front of the canal and behind it, since there was a possibility that the VC might come from our rear. By 2300 we were all in position and started the long wait. But we did not wait long. About 30 minutes later, to the flank and about 100 meters from where I was, there was a series of shots fired. I figured that some VC had run into our flank men, but I could not see down the canal, so I moved out of the bunker so that I could look down the canal. I felt that the VC would eventually attempt to cross the river. I also felt that this was probably only the advance security element of the larger force. I crawled into a good position beside the canal, and waited. In about 15 minutes I could just barely see a boat beginning to cross the river about 600–800 meters down the canal. This had to be the VC—no chance of civilians using the canal at a time like this—so I opened fire. I saw the boat flounder and some water splash, but it was just too dark and too far away to see more. I waited but no more VC attempted to cross. I believe the security elements had accomplished their mission—to warn the main VC force where we were and if we were there at all. We had no more activity all night but did hear dogs bark farther down the canal, which is a good sign that VC are in the area, and the main VC force probably crossed the canal far down from where we were. It was too bad that we did not really catch them, but you have to give the VC a little credit—they are pretty good fighters themselves and it is unusual to really catch them in an ambush. At 0600 in the morning we packed up and departed. We looked over the area real well, saw some blood, so we knew we wounded a couple. They never leave dead or wounded after a battle, so it is difficult to tell if we killed any of the three or four we saw. It was a good patrol, and we were all anxious to go on more. I have worked very close with the District S-2, and we have learned much from each other. I gave him a real good critique after we returned. I think I know a bit about night patrols, after about 50 of them in Ranger school.

BUILDER 2ND CLASS MARK W. HARMS *wrote many letters home to his parents while serving with the U.S. Navy Seabees from April 1968 to March 1969. He worked on civil action projects with a crew of Vietnamese civilians and was part of a team that responded immediately to all rocket attacks at Camp Books for rescue, cleanup, and salvage. His crew also built the Hoa Kahn Medical Clinic, where he also helped out on Sundays and time off duty. The clinic operates today as a mental hospital with over 500 patients.*

*This letter was written to his parents, Mr. and Mrs. Walter Harms, in Boring, Oregon.*

July 26, 1968

Dear Mom and Dad,

This is the first chance I've had to write you since the terrible night of the 24th of July. I never thought I would see the day when I was yelling for corpsmen or dragging wounded from the wreckage. It all started at 1917 o'clock. I was in the shower starting to shave. There was a loud scream and crash. I saw a big ball of fire and then I was flying through the air, I hit the door, and fell on my back. I rolled over and got on my knees and crawled for the bunker as fast as I could go. I no sooner got in the bunker and heard yells for help. Voils and I went outside and dragged Seiber in the bunker, covered with blood. I wrapped my towel around his foot and Callabressy put his shirt around his arm. I ran out of the bunker, grabbed my pants and slipped on my shoes and ran for the hootch with my buddies in it. There were already some guys helping there, so I ran to the hootch that took the direct hit. A colored kid and I were digging around looking for wounded. The colored guy grabbed one end of some tin and I got the other and we turned it over. There was a guy with a hole in his back big enough to put a softball in. Both arms were gone and one leg gone. By this time I was scared to death and more or less sick. I went back to the hootch to see how my buddies were. They were lying on the floor waiting to be hauled away. I

*38*

never saw so much blood in all my life, and the smell was something else. I went back to the bunker and helped Voils, Lambert, and a couple Marines carry Seiber out of the bunker. We were then told to get back in the bunker. We stayed in the bunker until 2020 o'clock then we all crawled out. We were all scared to death and jumpy as rabbits. We sat around waiting for reports on who got it. Sieber, Fox, Barbee, Myros, Beerworth, Driver, and Brown were on the report. Brown was O.K., he was released with two flesh wounds, one in the wrist and one in the upper leg, and he was with us when we got the report. We didn't know their conditions. We sat in the bunker most of the night, few of us slept. Voils and I sat by a pool of blood and didn't sleep at all. At 0400 Lambert, Callabressy, Taylor, and I went back in the hootch and sat on our racks. At 0630 we went to the shop and held muster. The chief sent Wilson, Brown, Kaminski, Freeman, Voils, and me to clean out the Seabee hootch. I can't describe the mess or how we got the place cleaned up, it's just too terrible. About all I can say is it was hell! Blood on the deck in pools, blood on racks, lockers, walls, ceiling, and everything else. There were hundreds of holes in everything. It smelled like warmed over death in a slaughter house. Every one of us were a little sick, scared, tired, and very jumpy. It took us till noon to get everything cleaned up and put all the gear in a safe place. The China Beach Public Works came in and started rebuilding because the commander thought we had been through too much to rebuild everything. We went back to our other jobs, but no one worked very hard. We were all waiting for more reports on our buddies. At 1610 o'clock the reports came in. They read as follows: Sieber, shrapnel left ankle and left wrist; Barbee, shrapnel hip, side, shoulder, and right leg; Driver, shrapnel right lower leg and groin; Myros, right upper arm, right forearm bones broken (compound), right upper leg broken; Beerworth, face wounds, jaw broken, shrapnel imbedded near brain; Fox, right side of face crushed, lost right eye, lost right elbow, shrapnel in right hip, shrapnel in spine, paralyzed from the waist down.

By 1730 o'clock we were on our way to 95th Evac hospital to see the guys. We got to talk to all of them and left at 2000 o'clock. It was a relief to see they would all make it. About 2010 we had a flat tire and had no spare. It took until 2230 to get a tire and by that time the roads were closed. We got to Tein Shaw at 2330 and ate and got about four hours sleep and headed back to Red Beach. We worked our regular jobs today and now I have watch tonight. That's the exact happenings. No heroes, everyone did their part and everyone was scared to death. I'm very thankful to be alive along with the other four guys in the shower. The rocket hit exactly 20 feet from the shower, and if it would have hit 10 feet farther left we would all be dead. Right now I'm still shook and would like very much to get out of here but that can't be done so all I can do is pray. All I got in the way of wounds were skinned-up feet and cut hand from crawling out of the shower. My right toe got infection in it but that's about it. I could have never written this letter yesterday and probably couldn't do it tomorrow or another time, the time just happens to be right. Please don't worry about me. It won't do any good and you can be darned sure I'm being careful.

Love,

Mark

P.S. Please send this to Jay, I don't think I can write another to send to anyone.

*The battle of the Ia Drang Valley, which took place in mid-November of 1965, was one of the hardest fought and most bloody of the entire war. The letter that follows is* SP-4 KENNETH W. BAGBY's *personal account of the action during that fierce encounter, written soon afterward to his parents in Winchester, Virginia.*

Nov. 17, 1965
Plei-Ku, Vietnam

Dear Folks,

I met a boy on the ship coming over to Vietnam. He was a good guy from the State of Missouri. He was my friend. We lived in the same tent together, went into An Khe together, and spent most of our free time together. I got to know this boy well, and he was my best friend. His name was Dan Davis.

On Monday morning, the 15th of November, he died in my arms of two bullet wounds in the chest. He said, "Ken, I can't breathe." There was nothing I could do.

To the right of me another friend, whose last name was Balango, died of a wound in the throat. Up front Sergeant Brown, my squad leader, was hit in the chest and leg. To my left Sp-4 A. Learn was hit in the ankle.

We were crossing a field and were pinned down by automatic weapons fire from the enemy. We were pinned down for about 45 minutes before the rest of the platoon could get to us, and save the rest of us.

So went the biggest and worst battle that any American force has had in Vietnam. We outdone the Marines and Airborne by a long shot. Estimated VC killed, 2,000. Our casualties, I cannot give the information out. The battle took place on the Cambodian border.

In another line of attack my platoon leader Lieutenant Marm was shot in the neck right beside me, about ten feet to my right. Me

*41*

and Sp-4 Ahewan took him back through the lines to the aid station.

Another situation, me, Daily, and Sergeant Riley captured two VC and were bringing them back through the lines when we were pinned down again, as one of them spotted a buddy and tried to signal him. I was going to kill both of them but Sergeant Riley stopped me.

Our battalion, the 1st BN 7th Cav., is completely inactive due to the killed and wounded of its men. My squad, which consists of nine men, three came out, myself, Sergeant Scott, and a boy named Stidell.

Folks, by all rights I should be dead. The good Lord evidently saw fit to spare me, for some reason. I prayed, and prayed and prayed some more, the three days we were in battle.

The many men that died, I will never forget. The odor of blood and decayed bodies, I will never forget. I am all right. I will never be the same though, never, never, never. If I have to go into battle again, if I am not killed, I will come out insane. I cannot see and go through it again. I know I can't. The friends I lost and the many bodies I carried back to the helicopters to be lifted out, I will never forget.

The pen that I am writing this letter with belongs to Stash Arrows, the boy that rode up to Winchester with me, on my emergency leave. Pop, remember him? He was hit three times in the back. I don't know if he is still alive or not. I hope and pray he is. God, I hope so.

Folks, don't let these men die in vain. Appreciate what they are doing over here in Vietnam. They died protecting you all, and all the people in the United States. We just cannot have the enemy get to the folks back home. We have got to stop them here, before that happens. If it is God's will, we will do it. Tell the people back home to pray for us, as we need their prayers. . . .

We raised the American flag on the grounds. We were fighting on Tuesday, the 16th of November. It waved proudly for the Armed Forces and the people of America, as it did in so many battles won in World War II and Korea. I sat beside a tree and looked at it, and hoped I would never see the day it would be torn down and destroyed.

Folks, I am glad Eddy is not here and my son Kenny is not here. I hope they never have to see or experience the horrors of war. I will give my life to see that they don't. . . .

As always,
Your son,
Kenneth

COLONEL ROBERT E. TSCHAN *wrote the following letters to his then–pen pal, now wife, Kathryn H. Deising, from January 1968 to September 1968. A captain in the U.S. Marine Corps, Colonel Tschan served in Vietnam from March 1967 to September 1968 as an advisor to Vietnamese Army units and was assigned to the U.S. Military Assistance Command-Vietnam (USMAC-V). His honors include the Bronze Star with Combat V and the Vietnamese Honor Medal, First Class. Upon his return to the U.S., he served as Acting Inspector General of the Marine Corps, and Chief of Staff, Marine Corps Air Ground Combat Center, in Twenty-Nine Palms, California.*

19 February '68

Dear Dee,

If you still have that article about the role and frustrations of an advisor to the Vietnamese, after my tour here—especially after the past two weeks—I bet I could tell them a few tales that would shake them up.

I wrote you a letter two wks. ago, but never got a chance to mail it. Just after I finished writing it, one of our senior advisors—my old assistant—was wounded. I flew out here to take over while he is treated, recuperates, and is able to return. "Here" is "Alpha One" outpost—the easternmost strongpoint in "McNamara's Wall," located 2000 meters south of the demilitarized zone and 4000 meters inland from the coast.

Being directly astride one of the NVA infiltration routes and also a stationary outpost, the NVA artillery above the Ben Hai River pounds us day and night. Our mission of course is to halt the NVA infiltration in this area. We live in heavily fortified bunkers, but this doesn't always help.

I had two other members on my advisor team but on our last operation, Bill, my Australian Warrant Officer, was wounded by a bullet through the wrist. That left me with myself and Sgt. Green as advisors. I had four naval gunfire people and two artillery forward observers attached to me.

We had two bunkers—one with Sgt. Green, the two artillery F.O.'s, and myself. The other bunker contained the four naval gunfire people.

On the third day after my arrival here we took a tremendous amount of "incoming" artillery. The two artillery F.O.'s were sleeping in my bunker. I was lying on my rack between them. Sgt. Green was standing at the other end of the bunker near the entrance.

Just after the incoming began, one of the naval gunfire men ran into my bunker and shouted, "Captain, our bunker just took a direct hit." He had a four-inch gash in his thigh. I jumped from my rack to go to the naval gunfire bunker. As I reached the entrance of my bunker, we took a direct hit from a 130mm artillery round with a delay fuse. It came clear through the roof and exploded directly under my rack, killing both of my artillery F.O.'s (the naval gunfire people are U.S. Marines—the artillery F.O.'s are U.S. Army).

In less than one minute, a relatively peaceful day went straight to hell. All four of my naval gunfire people were wounded—two seriously, my artillery personnel were dead. One of the naval gunfire people—Sgt. Holland, 22 yrs. old—was due to return to the U.S. yesterday and to be married next week. His leg is still buried among the shrapnel and debris of the bunker.

I immediately called for an emergency medevac helicopter. Miraculously, neither Sgt. Green nor I were wounded. After calling for the medevac chopper, I ran to see my counterpart (the Vietnamese battalion commander) to ask for assistance in carrying my dead and wounded to the landing zone so they could be picked up by the medevac choppers. The NVA artillery was still coming in but the goddamn Vietnamese would not come out of their bunkers to help us. Sgt. Green and I made six trips to the landing zone 200 meters away carrying our six dead and wounded.

The Vietnamese would not come out of their bunkers to help with the medevacs, but while Sgt. Green and I were loading the medevacs on the choppers, the bastards came out, went into our two bunkers and stole everything we owned, personal property, clothes, food, cigarettes, personal gear of our dead and wounded, and two $15,000 radios. Our sole purpose is to help them with their support, devace, air power, naval gunfire, artillery, and advice—and this is our reward.

Ask me what I think of the Vietnamese people and how I enjoy working with them!! This happened to me once before while I was serving as an advisor to another Vietnamese battalion. Please excuse my language. I still haven't calmed down. I hope you don't mind me telling you all this, but I must tell someone. I can't sit down and cry like I feel like doing due to my position. My relatives think I have a nice safe desk job and I can't tell them what I'm doing.

I have really had the Vietnamese up to here! I sometimes regret having extended, but I guess if I'm going to get that trip I want, I'm going to have to pay for it somehow.

Things have calmed down somewhat now. We have our bunker rebuilt to some degree of safety and I have a new naval gunfire team and a new artillery forward observer team. I guess I've cried on your shoulder long enough now. Your shoulder sure came in handy.

You asked about the competency of the advisory personnel. If I told you the true situation, I'd only seem like bragging and be accused of indulging in a petty jealousy which exists between the Marine Corps and the Army. I will brag to this extent, however, our particular advisor team—that which advises the 1st ARVN Infantry Division—has been awarded the U.S. Presidential Unit Citation for our accomplishments during this past year. Enough said.

As for my leave, having the travel time included in the six months extension would be outstanding, but I'm afraid I'm asking a bit too much. I will be due to return to the good ole U.S. during the first week of Nov.

I certainly wish I knew where I was going to be sent for my next duty station, but it will probably be sometime in Sept. before I know. One thing I do know is that they can't send me to another overseas station—can they? I've been overseas since April of '65 and am definitely looking forward to a decent stateside tour. Just think, American girls, American food, American cities, houses, cars, highways, restaurants, theaters, etc. Almost too good to imagine.

Don't stop writing now. I enjoy your letters very much. I don't get a chance to write too often and I'm not really sure when I'll be able to mail this letter. The only way in and out of this outpost is by helicopter—so on the next medevac or resupply helicopter I'll send this out. Hopefully on a resupply chopper.

Don't let those taxes get you down—you're paying my salary, and I really feel as if I've earned it this month.

Bob

P.S. I'd be happy to have you send "Doc" and your roommates to me—however, I don't know what the hell I'll do with a dog.

LIEUTENANT JOHN S. TAYLOR *wrote many letters home while serving two tours in 1968 and 1969 on board the USS* Boston *off North and South Vietnam. Initially an Assistant Damage Control Assistant, he was promoted to Gunfire Liaison Officer and then lieutenant (junior grade). Upon his release from active duty in 1970, Lieutenant Taylor joined the Vietnam Veterans Against the War (VVAW).*

*The following letters were sent to his parents, Mr. and Mrs. Frank D. Taylor, at the United States Embassy in Madrid, Spain, where his father was stationed as a Foreign Service Officer.*

May 10, 1968

This is no little picnic out here and I'm not trying to sound like a dashing hero. We've been shot at every day (except today, though the night is young and we're off to make a run at the beach with our small guns) since I've joined the ship. The first day I was here a couple of *real* near misses sent shrapnel whizzing about, wounding one man topside (they are using air bursting shells as well as the impact detonating type). We haven't been hit yet but the action we've been in warrants that sooner or later we'll get clunked. Those bunkers are getting pretty good and we can't seem to knock them out with our eight-inch guns or air strikes. We're right off the DMZ on the 17th parallel about 3–5 miles from Cap Lay. If it's as tense as this, being fired at from the shore batteries three miles away, think what it must be like on the ground.

June 18, 1968

As you may have read, we've been seeing a little action the past few nights. Saturday night we were fired at by an unidentified aircraft, either a Mig or helicopters, and had three near misses by rockets. Sunday night we were again attacked and a Mig scored a direct hit amidships, although the damage was not serious—a lot of bent and twisted railings and stuff like that—it didn't even penetrate the ship. But 20 miles north of us the Australian destroyer *Hobart*, who

Enclosed is part of the "Plan of the Day" to give you an idea of the "real NAVY.
I don't believe the EXECUTIVE OFFICER had the nerve to actually put this thing out.

Tuesday, June 18

Dear Mom + Dad,

As you may have head we've been seeing a little action the past few nights Saturday night we were fired at by an unidentified aircraft either a M16 or helicopters And has 3 near misses by rockets.

Sunday night we were again attacked and a MIG scored a direct hit amidships with a rocket, although the damage was not serious – a lot of bent and twisted railings and stuff like that – it didn't even penetrate into the ship. But 20 miles north of us the Australian destroyer HOBART, who sailed out here from Subic Bay with us, was heavily damaged by an air attack and lost 2 men and 7 wounded. An American destroyer with her was also hit but not hurt. (Don't believe this "stray missile" theory) Last night we all went to General Quarters again because of an erroneous report from one of the lookouts that 3 rockets missed us back aft. It turned out to be tracer fire or flares on the beach but there were still reports of an unidentified high speed aircraft in the vicinity that we

*Letter from John Taylor*

sailed out here from Subic Bay with us, was heavily damaged by an air attack and lost two men and seven wounded. An American destroyer with her (USS *Edson)* was also hit but not hurt. (Don't believe this "stray missile" theory.) Last night we went to General Quarters again because of an erroneous report that three rockets missed us back aft. It turned out to be tracer fire or flares on the beach but there were still reports of an unidentified high-speed aircraft in the vicinity that we periodically tracked then lost. It's really scary when you realize how ill-equipped we are to cope with any kind of air attack. The missiles are obsolete and the radar is inadequate. Yikes. In spite of these recent air attacks and the constant shelling of Saigon, we're winning this war. "Westy" says we've never been stronger and the enemy's morale and drive never lower. We've already shot more rounds (in the same area) these last two months than we did all last cruise off Vietnam. Somehow, that's not much to brag about—it seems to me that there is a definite lack of progress on the Front under these circumstances and that *perhaps* we're not as close as we might like to think we are to winning this war (Oh, no, it's not a "war," is it? Perhaps "conflict" is more correct since war was never declared on anyone). Ah, well, some fine day this conflict will be over and all the GIs can come back from the mountains, caves, and paddies, even though their welcome home won't be like VE Day or VJ Day. People will embarrassedly turn their heads when one of the Purple Heart winners goes by, knowing that he suffered in vain—no matter what the outcome of the Paris talks might be. It's just not the same as WWII, or even the Korean War. All these lies about how we're winning in the battlefields and about what a great job we're doing on the *Boston.* We blasted a pagoda a couple of days ago for *target practice*—I know, I was standing watch in the gun plotting room—and the captain comes over the loudspeaker that evening and says that we knocked out a pagoda which was sheltering North Vietnamese troops. Blasted lies and propaganda being fed to us and the public at every turn but no one pays any mind to the dissenting or questioning journalists or intellectuals because they're obviously "soft on Communism." It looks definite that we will be coming back out here again next year. I'd say that reflects a touch of concern and lack of optimism over the war's progress.

July 6

Things are really booming (ha ha) around here—we're in the tag-end of Operation Thor, a combined land, sea, and air push against the NVA around the DMZ. We bang away all night (three-gun salvos from the big babies), rapid fire then pull out to rearm during the morning and afternoon. The B-52s have been plastering the areas in the northern part of the DMZ, and the Marines and ARVN have been busy on the beach. There are all sorts of ships around us—four destroyers and the *St. Paul* and the *Providence,* both cruisers. When we leave the firing line, the *St. Paul* takes our place. At the moment, we are rearming from the *Haleakala,* and later afternoon we're taking on oil from the *Camden.* I stand watches in Weapons Control these days. I act as coordinator with the Marine spotter on the beach and relay gun adjustments (right 200 yds, drop 50, etc.) on the targets until we get zeroed in. We just kick up a lot of dirt trying to knock out these coastal defense sites—not even the B-52s seem to be effective—there are more now than four years ago. We just keep them hopping and blast away at road junctions, river crossings, and fortified villages in unobserved H&I (Harassment & Interdiction) shoots to keep troops and supplies from moving about too freely in the DMZ. That area looks like the face of the moon, it's so bullet-ridden. But nothing makes those guys pull out. I'll tell you, though, the B-52s must really shake those NVA artillery men up a bit with their 1000 and 2000 lb. bombs. We could feel the concussion of those things going off *seven* miles off the beach. The smoke and dirt rose thousands of feet in the air after one of their attacks—it must be quite unpleasant for the troops manning those shore battery emplacements, that's all I can say. In two days we're going back to Subic Bay to get new barrels on all the eight-inch and five-inch guns. On some, the wear is over *100%*. So you can imagine the kind of accuracy we've got these days. We've got a mail helo coming this afternoon so I'll get this off.

WO-1 RICHARD ELLIOT *(1st Cavalry Division)* of Clearwater, *Florida, describes his battle experience in these excerpts from letters written to his father.*

April 1966

. . . Nothing much has been happening. It is pretty dull now. Our job is done. We found the Cong, now the division has to kill them off. Yesterday we caught a hundred or so in the open. We bombed them, then our gunships went in and cut them down. I had to sit back here with the lift section and listen to all the fun, I didn't get to kill one. We captured a 75mm recoilless rifle, though. . . .

We took a Special Forces team out the other day. . . . They ran into some trouble, and we had to pick them up early. When we got them, one mountain tribesman came running up to the ship with a Viet Cong head in his hand. . . .

We are moving farther north tomorrow. Start trying to find Charlie again. Maybe this time I'll get to kill some.

We moved, and now we are about 40 miles north of Plei-Ku. . . .

I wonder if all these guys get scared. Every time I go into an area my stomach ties into a knot. It is the idea of just having to sit there like a bull's-eye while the troops get off, and not being able to fire back . . .

July 1966

Still here. I think we'll stay here quite a while, also. The more we look the more we find.

I went on the ground again yesterday, and we came upon a VC training center and first-aid area. The Cong must have moved out when they heard us coming, for they left gear and warm chow laying around. We searched the buildings. This done, we headed up the trail the Cong used to leave by.

I was in the lead squad, about third man back. The point man signaled for us to stop, and we crouched there looking up the trail. I guess this was too much for the Cong, because four or five of them broke and ran from about 20 feet in front of us. We shot at them but didn't hit any. That jungle is so thick it makes it hard. I caught a glimpse of one running through the brush and fired a burst at him from my M-16. Must have missed him by a mile. Sure feels funny to shoot at a human being.

We followed them a short way, but figured they might be trying to lead us into an ambush, so we turned back.

Today we dropped our blues into an area they were in two days ago. They killed four Cong and found a big system of tunnels and caves. Today they went back with blasting equipment. Boy, are they going to fix those tunnels. . . .

SPECIALIST 5TH CLASS BILL MCCLOUD *served in Vietnam from March 1968 to March 1969 as flight operations coordinator with the 147th Assault Support Helicopter Company at the air base in Vung Tau. He is the author of* What Should We Tell Our Children About Vietnam?

*He wrote the following letter to his mother, Joyce McCloud, of Ponca City, Oklahoma, detailing the thrill he found in flying on missions.*

18 Jan 69
Sat. Morn.

Dear Mom—

I went flying January 5th and we had a very long day. We got 15½ hours in the air; 5½ hours of it was night combat assault. Most of our flying time over here is considered direct combat support. But for those 5½ hours we were resupplying a front-line unit that was in direct contact and fighting with the enemy at the time and we were flying right against known enemy positions. We carried about seven loads in and received heavy enemy fire the first three times, but did not take any hits. We were resupplying a 9th Infantry Division company who had a VC company pinned down, who, in turn, had another U.S. company pinned down. This was one day when there was no doubt in my mind that there is a war going on here.

We left at 8:15 in the morning and returned at 1:30 the next morning. I got to see a lot of the delta region of Vietnam. We flew down to the southern tip of Vietnam, to the extreme western border next to the sea, and northwest to where we were less than 10 miles from the Cambodian border. We covered the entire IV Corps area of South Vietnam.

I was gunner on the right side for about seven hours, while the regular gunner got some sleep. During the combat assault at dark the regular gunner took over and I was the only one at the rear of the aircraft and had an M-14 sticking out one of the porthole windows.

We had quite an air drama the other night. It was about 8:00 at night and a voice came on the emergency frequency on the radio. He said he was in an LOH helicopter (which only has one pilot and one crew member, who is an enlisted man like myself). He said that the pilot had just been wounded and was unconscious and that he was at the controls of a helicopter for the first time. He requested instructions from someone so he could land the ship. Another helicopter flying in the area heard him and started giving him instructions as to what to do with his left hand and his right hand. The entire thing lasted for about 30 minutes and I was able to hear both sides of the conversation the entire time. It was thrilling and he landed it like he had been flying for 20 years.

We had a man killed about 1:00 yesterday morning in a freak, unnecessary accident. He was lying on top of an aircraft, checking for an oil leak while the aircraft was running, and for some unknown reason he raised up right into the moving rotor blades and was knocked to the ground. He was DOA at the hospital, of a concussion they think. There was no blood. It can only be blamed on himself, but try to explain that to his pregnant wife who he was going home to in May.

I'll write again in a few days.

Love,
Billy

*In early August 1968 the 1st Brigade of the 101st Airborne Division made an assault into the Ashau Valley, west of Hue.* CHAPLAIN BILL LIBBY *accompanied the 2nd Battalion, 502nd Infantry on the assault and remained with them for a number of days. The following letter to his wife was written over several days and describes the operation.*

Tues. 6 Aug. 1968

Dear Babe—

A quick résumé of the past few days—exciting and tearing as it has been. Friday and Saturday I got my things together—made sure my rucksack was in good shape. Saturday morning I went to Co D, 2/502 Inf., with whom I was to make the assault. I got my four day ration of C's and LRRP rations (dehydrated, but very good) and packed it in with one extra pair of socks, my foot powder (Dr Scholl's from Mom Dunkle) and my water purification tablets. About 1500 the 800 of us from the 2/502 moved by truck about seven miles out into the jungle to spend the night. Another battalion, the 2/327, with whom Ray Hunt was to go, was camped right next to us. They were to go at 0830, and us at 1100. If you get a National Geographic RVN map—maybe you can find these places. We were scheduled for A Luoi Air Field in the northern end of the Valley and the 2/327 at Tabat in the south. On Sunday morning there was heavy fog at Tabat, so at 0830 we were told to get our packs on. At 0900 came the biggest collection of choppers I have ever seen. These 60 Hueys for carrying us in—two companies at a time—about 15–20 gunships for protection and two or three medevacs just sitting by. D and B went in first to secure the LZ, so I went in early.

0815 Thurs. 8 Aug.

What an unbelievable night! We moved into a position yesterday for the night—it turns out to be the middle of an NVA Base Camp—but they had gone, only the rear elements here—but that was bad enough. About 20 minutes after we got here an NVA Lt. walked up to the perimeter to surrender, but before we understood, one of the boys shot him in the leg. We tried to get him out for questioning last night but the chopper kept getting shot at. So this morning our men have cleared the area and the birds are overhead now—three gunships and a passenger ship. The Lt. is in a sling and they are going to pull him up. The chopper just went down in flames—must go help.

40 minutes later

One of the covering gunships took ground fire, flipped over and crashed. Three of the four crew men are dead—we have been able to check now that the fuel has stopped burning. A platoon is looking for the fourth, as he may have been thrown out.

To clarify a little, I stayed with D Co—Sat., Sun., and Monday. Monday night I switched to A Co, and have been there since. It has been one long fight ever since. I travel with the Co CP, which is in the middle so I'm relatively safe. Last night we got hardly any sleep. Our troops knew they had to be quiet and not fire for fear of giving their positions away. Then they would have been hit with RPGs, so our fellows threw grenades and our artillery was fired as close to us as possible. The CO was very edgy and we sat and talked in whispers for a long time.

The fourth crewman has been found, and all the bodies brought in. This sort of thing causes some resentment among our fellows as they feel the lives of four U.S. troops can't be counted against one NVA prisoner. However, that is only a relative question when judged in nationalistic terms. If we didn't keep them from it, some would certainly try to kill him with little or no feeling.

Everyone is depressed right now and probably will be for a while. Two other companies are now moving through the jungle toward us and will join us later today. Then together the whole area will be cleared and the POW and bodies lifted out.

Some of the things I've learned—water is very important. The men can go without food for three or four days, but one day without water and we start having heat exhaustion.

Fri 9th

Am in my own tent. Came in this morning with bodies from chopper. Will visit hospitals, then go back tonight. . . .

Love,

Bill

CORPORAL COTTRELL FOX *sent the following letter home to his parents, Cottrell and Dorothy Fox, in St. Louis, Missouri. It was written from the 91st Evacuation Hospital at Cam Ranh Bay after he was wounded on the first day of the Tet Offensive. Corporal Fox arrived in Vietnam in February 1967 and was initially assigned to Headquarter 3rd Tank Battalion as an interpreter and then volunteered as a rifleman in the 3rd Combined Action Group. His platoon, Hotel 8, was located in Loc Dien village, approximately fourteen miles south of the city of Hue. His honors include the Vietnamese Cross of Gallantry and the Purple Heart. The 3rd Combined Action Group was awarded both the Naval Unit Citation and a Presidential Unit Citation for achievements during the Tet Offensive.*

Feb. 2, 1968
Cam Ranh Bay

Dear Mom and Dad:

Well, here I am at the U.S. Air Force Hospital in beautiful Cam Ranh Bay. I've got lacerations of the scalp, a ringing in my ears, a bullet hole in my right arm, and frag wounds over my whole lower body—my left leg looks like a model of the surface of the moon. How did all this come to pass? On the night of 31 Jan. Hotel 8 was attacked by an estimated 400 VC with mortars, rockets, ground assault, sappers, and *gas*. The attack started at 4:00 A.M. We suffered two Marines and three PFs dead and every Marine in the compound wounded. Additionally there were beaucoup PFs wounded. We had four VC bodies left in the compound plus over 100 undetonated satchel charges, Chi Com grenades, AK-47 magazines, holster and belt, pistol magazines, gook gas, grenades, B-40 rockets, gook packs, gook gas masks, ammo, an AK-47 rifle, and undoubtedly a hell of a lot more gear that has been collected since I left on the morning of 31 Jan. Before I left I heard over the radio that the grunts sweeping across the tracks had found 25 NVA bodies that had been hastily abandoned. Additionally, Capt. Hall told me that as of two o'clock in the afternoon of the 31st the grunts already had killed 12 fleeing gooks and were still in very heavy contact.

The gooks held a large part of our compound, maybe three-quarters, for about an hour—there were about 75–100 actually in there with us. They had three 82mm mortars, at least, and they put over 200 rounds into our little area. It was the most unbelievable night that I'll ever spend. I've never really thought that I was going to die before, but that night I truly believed that I would. It was hell as no civilian and hardly any Marine can imagine. No words can de-scribe it and no one can begin to appreciate it unless he has lived through a similar situation. Firefights and heavy contact are not even in the same league. This is something special. I have never fought so hard in my life. I have never wanted to see dawn break so badly.

This was, to understate it, the most intense experience of my life. It has taken me a couple of days to get up the gumption to write about it. I do not write about it happily because I'm very weary of war—although I enjoy it while the shooting is going on. If I could just blow gooks away and then forget about it for a few days it would be great. I am writing to you all about it because I feel you deserve to know about it and because I know that later, if I make it home, that I will want some sort of record of what happened to me in the Nam. Here it is:

Feb. 3, 1968

I tried to write the story for you but I got so tired that I had to quit. It's worthy of a book, believe me. At this time I don't want to do it—I'm weary of thinking of it—it's nearly all I think of as it is. The experience beat the hell out of me. I'll try to write it in a few days. Briefly, 400 VC attacked us at 4:00 A.M. from all sides—maybe 100 penetrated the compound—mostly sappers. They wouldn't have gotten in except they tear-gassed us and really screwed our dope up. When that happened we had to fall back to the center of the compound around the radio bunker and the Abortion—an adjacent wooden bunker which we had just built and in which I slept. The M-60 was fouled with dirt when it was knocked out of Tyrell's hands so we didn't use it. Avery, our M-79 man, ran out the back door of his hootch with the 79 and was attacked by six gooks. He strangled one and broke away from the others but the 79 got lost in the process. Dories was in a bunker on the east side when the gooks shoved a satchel charge through the window—it went off, severing his arm and leg, collapsing the bunker on top of him. The bunker burned—he was unrecognizable the next morning when we pulled his body out of the rubble. Murray was in the same bunker but he got out before it blew. A gook shot him above the heart—however, he crawled around the hootches and into the unfinished wood bunker, the "Abortion," from which we were firing. We put him in my rack and Doc attended him but he died there. Grunder, who'd gotten back from special leave that day and taken the compound over from me, was in the radio bunker. He called for artillery all around our perimeter, and then when things got worse—on the compound itself. Finally, we called the deadliest antipersonnel arty of all in on ourselves—VT. VT is a variable line of fragmentation round that goes off 50 ft. above deck and sprays fragments 360 degrees on everything below it. We called in 20 rounds of the stuff plus 50 rounds of 155mm high explosive on the compound itself. We fired an additional 90 rounds into the graveyard, railroad tracks, back roads, villes, etc. It was unbelievable. All this time the gooks were mortaring, rocketing, grenading, satchel-charging, and shooting up our area.

They only used gas initially but I caught a big whiff of it and was staggering around crying and throwing up. I was the last man out of the area that they initially gassed—the north side. Eventually the stuff was all over the compound. I stumbled up to a small bunker in the middle of the compound trying to get clear of the gas—I was leaning on the bunker choking when a big pineapple Chi

Com bounced off my *head* and hit at my feet—I saw it lying there, its fuse sparking. I made a feeble attempt at running, got two feet, and it exploded, filling the backs of both my legs from the middle of my back down with hundreds of fragments of stone, dirt, sand, wood, and grenade—it nearly blew my trousers off. Gooks started shooting at me from the road and paddies—they blew the bolt and upper receiver out of my rifle. I got back to the Abortion, where Daniels, Doc, and Grissom were. Dan and Doc had .45s and grenades only but the pistols turned out to be great. Mortar fire was so thick that every time you moved anywhere you were picked up and knocked down, maybe two, three, or four times. Grissom was firing out the door when a mortar wounded him. I took his rifle and he, Thang (a wounded PF), and Doc filled magazines for me. We guarded the doors and two firing ports of the bunker and each time the gooks tried to assault us we'd blow them away. They kept throwing blocks of explosives at us from over the hootches. We threw 20 grenades back there and all around us and then ran out of grenades. The grenades were saving us so I had to get more. I sprinted out to a trench, got a case of 30, and ran back. The gooks shot a B-40 rocket at me that missed and hit the chow hall, setting it afire. About this time the arty started coming in and it really screwed the gooks' dope up. I could hear them in the compound and outside the perimeter getting ready for a final assault, but when the big stuff started coming in, they broke and ran. Brown, who was on the road in Bunker 4, was taking a tremendous volume of fire from the railroad tracks across the paddy and a lot of rocket fire from two big graves next to the tracks in the paddy. The gooks were coming over the paddy wire on bamboo mats and cutting the wire and crawling through, when two rounds of VT burst directly over them. He said he saw nothing but gooks beating feet, dragging their dead and wounded back with them. The stuff was bursting directly over our bunker but as long as we stayed in it we were okay. It made the weirdest, most beautiful metallic sound in the world when it burst.

My rifle was so hot now that I had to take off my shirt and hold the forestock with it. A number of times the gooks' AK fire would get so nasty that I'd just stick the rifle out the door without looking and blow the whole magazine on automatic. Near the end, by the volume of fire, I could tell the gooks were withdrawing from the south end of the compound, the end which I was firing at. I stuck my head and shoulders out, pulled off half a magazine, and caught a carbine round in the muscle of my right arm. I even saw the son of a bitch that shot me. He was firing automatic from the corner of Bunker 2. The wound didn't even hurt—I thought I'd just caught a wood splinter. Grissom extended a KAW (rocket) for me and I shot it at the corner of Bunker 2, blowing my gooney friend into Valhalla or wherever dead gooks go. His friends dragged his remains off but I did find plenty of his body and body fluids so that I can be pretty sure I got him. In addition, we found the stock of his carbine. Chalk up another probable for me.

We kept praying for dawn to break—and it seemed it took forever. We took sporadic fire right up until light came, and then the gooks pulled back into the villes, but not very far, for when the grunts went out there they ran into beaucoup goonies who were covering the retreat and trying to treat their wounded and bury their dead. The grunts, I heard, found 25 bodies that we had killed. I know there were beaucoup dead—everywhere you shot you hit them. You could see them fall and hear them crying. When dawn broke we had two dead Marines, and three dead PFs. Doi lay dead on Bunker 3 in the parapet—shot in the back of his head. Another, Chuc, lay dead in the trench next to 3—he'd been overrun. A third was killed by a satchel charge thrown into the bunker where he was sleeping.

The chow hall, the Doc's hootch (aid station) Bunker 5, the bunker Dories was killed in, Bunker 1, the Mayor's office, Tyrell's sleeping bunker, were all finished—totaled. The two Marine hardbacks were badly damaged but didn't burn. None of my gear was scratched! I even took a whole roll of color film with my camera that morning—flicks of the compound so that you can understand exactly what happened.

Bunker 4 was damaged—the tin roof of the parapet looked like it had been opened with a giant can opener. The radio bunker had the two nine two (292) aerial blown off and the back side was scorched (it abutted the now smoldering chow hall but was otherwise okay). Bunkers 3 and 2 were okay, as were the rest of the bunkers. The damage wasn't nearly as bad as that done at Hotels 6 and 7. Furthermore, we had held our compound and kicked the gook's tail (pardon the French). Virtually everyone crawled out of their positions smiling, chuckling to themselves and feeling around to see if anything vital was missing. Never has such joy shone on my face as when I emerged from the Abortion that morn. The feeling was one of true exultation. Yes, despite gas, that Chi Com actually bouncing off my head and exploding at my feet, mortars, TNT, rifle fire, and our own people and artillery, I'm actually alive and in one piece! It was the greatest day of my life.

The feeling passed as I made my way to Bunker 4—Charlie Brown's bunker—he and I had been in voice contact until 45 mins. before dawn, when I heard his last yells. I crept up there fearing the worst. I had seen fire coming from the bunker even though I couldn't communicate with him. I thought maybe he was dead and a PF had his rifle. I stuck my head in the door and lo and behold there he was laying on a rack bleeding through a battle dressing on his leg, with the same sort of crazy grin as I had on my face. We could have kissed each other, believe me. He had a huge bullet hole in his leg but was in great spirits. Gordon had been with him and the two of them had fought like crazy and held the bunker. The two PFs with them were both wounded by shrapnel from B-40 rockets which had penetrated the walls of the bunker in three places—one, Dom, was shell-shocked! Charlie had been shot when he was running in and out of the bunker firing. The impact had been so great that it knocked and spun him about 10 ft. (right now he's in this very ward—this afternoon he's being shipped to a hospital in the Philippines—lucky dog!).

I was the only one looking around. I went very cautiously up to the northern end of the compound. I found Doi on his back, eyes open in disbelief—dead in the parapet of Bunker 3. Below him dead in a trench was Chuc. Both were good PFs. In a trench between the ammo bunker and Bunker 5, I found two bodies, still alive but wounded. One was dressed only in a loincloth (uniform of NVA sappers)—the other had on an NVA uniform. Neither had a weapon. Both were breathing. The gooks had left them there. They were resting, one on top of the other—one with his head on the other's stomach. The one in the loincloth raised up suddenly with a Chi Com in his hand. I was above and behind them both and blew each one's head off with a full magazine of tracers on auto. The one with the grenade bucked and jumped a good two feet into the air and fell back dead, the Chi Com still in his hand. Chalk up two more confirmeds for me, making a total of four. The shooting brought everybody out of their holes and all of us began searching. We found another dead NVA in the paddies on the west side of the road. The PFs crept down through the wire and got his AK-47 and a pack containing 15 AK-47 magazines, new ammo, ten grenades, and TNT. The PFs told me the dude had been wounded in the chest and was left behind when the goonies made their bird. He had come walking down the road yelling "Chieu Hoi, Chieu Hoi" (Surrender, Surrender) with his rifle over his head. Nien, the best PF we've got, saw him. At about 4:30, Nien had caught the blast of an 82 mortar full in the face—his cheek was hanging and his whole face was burnt and torn. When he saw this Chieu Hoi he blew him off the road over the wire and 10 ft. down the embankment into the paddy. Sorry about that. We found another body up the road about 250 meters north—he'd been killed by the variable time—that in itself was not amazing—what was newsworthy was the fact that he had

Grunder's rifle! Five or six gooks (sappers—almost unarmed except
for the TNT and satchel charges) had jumped him and grabbed his
rifle. They didn't get away with it.

Later, in a small bunker that had been blown, we heard faint
screams. After some desperate digging we uncovered Ha Si Nhut
(Cpl.) Su—one of the best PFs—he was burned and in shock. He
was medevacked with us. By this time the grunts from the two
bridges 500 and 900 meters to our south had arrived. They, too, had
been heavily hit—they had at least one KIA. Also, Hotel 3 brought
a squad down in a truck and medevacked all the dead and wounded
up to their position to wait medevac choppers. We dug Dories out
of the bunker, got our weapons together, and those of us who were
left were taken up to Hotel 3 and medevacked from there. I spent
the whole day at Alpha Med in Phu Bai. The number of Marines
and 1st Cav. Division casualties was tremendous. The gooks took
Hue, as I guess you heard. At 5:30 P.M., Phu Bai was rocketed, and
again at 9:00. That nearly shot my nerves—I was already weak from
loss of blood, no chow and water, but that really did it. I almost got
battle fatigue. A doctor did me a big favor by sending me down here
to Cam Ranh. It's unbelievable. I'm in an Air Force hospital that is
as good as anything—civilian or military—stateside. We have air-
conditioning, linoleum, stateside civilian type showers and bath-
rooms, great chow, TV, movies, everything. It's heaven. The people
are nice. We even have beaucoup nurses. The area and countryside
are very pleasant to the eye. Blacktop roads, sidewalks, green hills,
the bay and white sand . . . no dirt or dust. It's nothing like up north
at all. I guess you've heard the gooks have gone ape. We are getting
over 200 casualties here at night. It's unbelievable. I heard that
Hotels 4 and 5 and Phu Loc headquarters have been overrun—that
from a new arrival. I cannot judge the veracity of the report but it
sounds reasonable.

I have no idea how long I'll be here. Probably for a number of
days. Right now the surgical staff only handles amputations and the

most serious wounds. There are hundreds and hundreds of bullet and shrapnel cases waiting to be operated on plus the regular non-battlefield cases. I may be here quite a while, but you never know. I've now got 44 days until I must be out of the field (18th), and 49 (the 23rd) until I *have* to be out of the country. If I go back to Phu Bai, which I'm sure I will—all I can say is, pray.

Well, my arm hurts like crazy so I'll have to go. Remember I'm O.K. and love to all.

Cot

P.S. I'm in Ward 14, 12th USAF Hospital, Cam Ranh Bay, Viet Nam, 96326. Write if you like but I may not get it here. Will write you again from here.

P.S.S. One of the nicer things that we discovered in the morning was that all our claymore wires had been cut. It was obvious that this was an "inside" job—one of our great PFs—just thought you'd be interested. Additionally, a PF Cpl. hid in our radio bunker the whole time—at the south end, the PF end, I heard little firing. Oh, what sterling allies!

CORPORAL JOHN O'HALLORAN *of Brooklyn, New York, describes some heavy fighting in this letter written as a private, to his father.*

18 July 1965

Dear Dad:

. . . Well guess what, I am in *Vietnam.* Today is Sunday, July 18, and I've been here since Wed., 14 July. That makes a total of four days so far spent in hell. Since I've been here I've been in one killing, and almost killed myself. Last Friday, July 16, we went on a fire mission into War Zone D (that's where there is nothing else but Viet Cong), and were under heavy mortar fire. Believe me, I was never so scared in all my life, seeing everything around me being blown up. Two guys were killed and seven more wounded. The Captain ordered a quick retreat, and those words sounded so good I could have kissed him.

Saturday was the worst day of all. I was one of the guys picked to go out on a patrol. . . . That was the most sickening day of my life. We were walking down a road, and coming from the opposite direction was a woman and a little baby in her arms. The Sergeant told us to watch out for a trap, because the VC use women all the time. We were maybe fifteen feet from her and she started crying like a baby. I didn't know what was going on, and the next thing I knew the Sergeant shot the hell out of the both of them. She had a grenade under the baby's blanket which was noticeable, but she was afraid to sacrifice her kid to kill us, so she started crying. The Sergeant said it's a dirty war, but it's kill or be killed.

This coming Wed. we are going on a six-day field mission into War Zone D that should be a wild battle. I am in Bien Hoa, five miles from the D zone. The temperature out here ranges from 100 to 133 degrees. Today the temperature is 117, and it's hot. I pull guard duty every night for two hours, so you don't get much sleep. The other night some VC tried to capture one of the Australians from their camp. They tried to drag him away but he blew the hell out of two of them and the others took off. We sleep in sandbag bunkers built next to our howitzers.

Well I guess that's about all for now, write soon. . . . I intend to buy a camera, so that I can take some pictures and show you what this jungle looks like. To prove to you how scared I am, I went to mass and confession today.

Hope to see you soon.

Love,

John

LANCE CORPORAL JOHN A. KRGA *arrived in Vietnam on May 19, 1969. He was sent to the 1st Marine Division, 7th Marine Regiment, 2nd Battalion, Hotel Company, weapons platoon, where he was assigned to 60mm mortars (0341). He was part of a battalion of four "watered-down companies" that, due to malaria and heat stroke, faced a superior force, the 2nd Division of the NVA, in places like Death Valley (Hiep Duc), Antenna Valley, and Pagoda Valley. Lance Corporal Krga received two medevacs in two months for two different strains of malaria and was sent home in November 1969 because of an anemic condition.*

*Lance Corporal Krga wrote the following letter home to his brother, Robert M. Krga, Jr., describing the first confrontation between the 7th Marines and the 2nd Division of the NVA in the sweltering Death Valley.*

Aug. 27, 1969

Dear Buzz,

I don't know where the fuck to begin. It all started about two days ago when we got choppered into this nameless valley to drag this one company out of the shit it got into. Well we did so without taking any casualties, they had three dead. Then yesterday the shit hit the fan. We had six KIAs in our company alone and about six wounded. The other three companies also got their ass kicked. These gooks are imbedded in these mountains and we can't get them out, neither can all the bombs and artillery they've been dropping on them constantly. The motherfuckers are still there. They've shot down two of our resupply choppers. Today is the 3rd day without food for us. I am so weak I can hardly walk. I am going crazy, Buzz, I really am. With all these air strikes and explosions constantly around us, the heat, no food, and the fact that these fucking gooks are still up there, is doing it to me. They almost had us (our whole battalion) surrounded yesterday. They choppered in another company to hold the rear, the only spot the gooks aren't yet. Now it's

Aug 27

**1ST MARINE DIVISION (REIN), FMF, VIETNAM.**

Dear Buzz,

I don't know where in the fuck to begin. It all started about 2 days ago when we got choppered into this nameless valley to drag this one company out of the shit it got into. Well, we did so without taking any casualties, they had 3 dead. Then, yesterday the shit hit the fan. We had 6 KIA's in our company alone and about 6 wounded. The other 3 companies also got their ass kicked. These gooks are imbedded in these mountains and we can't get them out, neither can all the bombs + artillery they've been dropping on them constantly. The mother-fuckers are still there. They've shot down 2 of our resupply choppers. Today is the 3rd day without food for us. I am so weak I can hardly walk. I am going crazy Buzz, I really am. With all these air strikes + explosions constantly around us th

*Letter from John Krga*

around 11 A.M. and they are buckling all around us, all over hell rounds are flying. Yesterday we were pinned down all day by snipers, it's really rough. We are somewhere North of Chu Lai, I think about 15 miles or so at the foot of the mountains. I don't know how long we'll be here or what but all we want right now is some fucking food. Well I've got to stop and try and sleep as I am weak and very tired. Please don't let Dad or Mom see this. I doubt if I will have time to write any more.

John

COLONEL RICHARD L. ST. JOHN *graduated from West Point in 1966 and went on to serve with the U.S. Army, 2nd Battalion (Airborne), 506th Infantry Regiment, 101st Airborne Division, from December 1967 to December 1968. He served in the Tet Offensive of 1968 and the Summer Offensive of the same year. His honors include the Silver Star, the Vietnamese Cross of Gallantry with Silver Star, and the Purple Heart. He is the author of* Circle of Helmets, *an account of his tour in Vietnam.*

*These letters were written from War Zone D while he was a first lieutenant with B Company (Tiger Bravo), 2nd Battalion (Airborne), 506th Infantry Regiment, and describe his first taste of combat.*

June 4, 1968

I'm now at the 6th Convalescent Center in Cam Ranh Bay. I hope that I won't be here long. . . . I go to see my doctor tomorrow to get the final word. . . . This place is right on the beach (I can't go in the water), has hot showers (I can't take a shower), has a snack bar, movies, library, PX, USO show . . .

. . . None of the tension has left me yet. I guess it will if I stay here any length of time. I just can't get over the fact that myself nor anyone else is walking around without a weapon. It has become a part of me the last six months and I just can't get used to it.

July 27, 1968

. . . We got lifted out of the battle site at 1530 yesterday because Charlie broke contact. We went straight into a combat assault north of Cu Chi. I got the company up at 0200 this morning because I had to be in position around a village at 0600. C, D, & B Companies are surrounding this village, with A Company searching it. A Company already has four or five casualties from booby traps and I have two. Platoon Sergeant Sykes was one of my wounded (both of mine are wounded). One was bad and Sykes wasn't too bad off.

. . . I still feel the same way. I want to get off the line. I'm tired of this war. Just so tired.

. . . The realization of what could happen has finally caught up with me.

July 28, 1968

Well, last night I took three more casualties from a booby trap. I've just about had it. The only thing that keeps me going is . . . the duty concept that West Point beat into me. That won't let me quit. My company is down to 82 people, I used to have four platoons but because I have lost so many people and leaders I have dropped to three platoons and they're all at half strength. This is the notorious dirty "nickel & dime stuff" that the VC are good at (nickel & dime meaning two or three casualties at a time).

Thank God I can hide my feelings and keep a stone face. Otherwise everyone would know how I feel. . . . Like I said, I still have my duty concept to keep me going, so my efficiency as a CO hasn't been touched, but I'm all torn up inside. I won't ever be lax or fall to pieces but I just want out.

. . . I hope I don't have anymore casualties today. They hit me very deeply in my heart when I see my people loaded on choppers killed or wounded.

August 6, 1968

Well, I'm 24! We didn't get to a fire support base last night. We went straight into another battle. Luckily we didn't see any action. A Company did and Matt has been wounded. He's not serious because I heard him on the radio a couple of hours after he was hit. What a birthday party. The sky was lit up by flares, tracers everywhere, air strikes, etc. I was up all night and right about midnight the battle was still going on. The gooks were shooting antiaircraft fire at helicopters, jets, anything. . . . The body count for the action on the 25th is now 78 gooks. Today's (actually last night's) is 16 so far.

# LIFE

*"Our base camp at Cu Chi has an odor*
*I don't think I'll ever forget.*
*It's a combination of red clay, tar, oil,*
*and heat, lots of heat!"*

SERGEANT GEORGE R. BASSETT *of Portland, Maine, wrote the following letter home to his parents detailing operations against hostile forces in the mountainous jungles of Tuy Hoa Province, Republic of Vietnam, against the 95th People's Army, North Vietnam.*

*Sergeant George Bassett, Jump School, 1964 (photo taken by fellow squad members with George's camera)*

21 Mar. 66
Tuy Hoa

Dear Dad, Mom & Kids:

I hope that you are all fine. Guess by now the winter must be leaving you.

Got three letters from you today, got about 11 altogether, and one from my buddy that was shot four times. He will be O.K. but won't walk for at least a year. Is 130 miles from home (Texas) in the hospital.

We are still in the mountains (jungle) and have set up a little camp so we can be resupplied and get mail and Red Cross items (cigs, soap, razors, insect repel). We get resupplied every three days, our rotation has been delayed until June as we ran into a lot more crap here than expected. We won't be out of the jungle til May 15, and then will head for base camp (P.R.). This is just like a real good war movie. For two days straight F-100s and B-57s and sky raiders have been bombing the side of this mountain we have been trying to go up. Our other two battalions (1st & 2nd-327) tried to get into this valley and never made it 200 m. and were pushed out. My company and C Co. tried and we walked in unopposed for about 20,000 m. We were on our way out and started running into the VC. Everything is going pretty well though. We are supposed to go about 10 mi. N on the 25th. I'm glad, as the leeches here are terrible, all over the ground and in the trees, always have three or four on you no matter how fast you pick them off. Too bad they weren't good to eat. Letters will probably be few and far between but don't let it worry you as we are in the boonies. In the box I sent were two dolls for that woman. Why don't you just give her one and send the other to Claudia Whitehurst. I promised her one but forgot to send it so please send her one of them.

We have been finding a lot of gold in the streams we have been crossing and following. Very small pieces but piles of it.

Just went out and took a couple pics. with my ½ frame camera (72 pics per roll) of the F-100s strafing the mountain in back of us. Those 20mm cannons sure make a horrible noise. Sounds like a metal ripping. Both legs of my pants are ripped from the crotch to knees, so I'm just hanging out getting a sunburn. These jungle fatigues always seem to rip there.

Sure am proud of Dick for doing so well on the basketball. Hope he keeps with it.

Any word yet on whether John will be coming up this summer? Sent camera in box, you can have it fixed and keep it. Costs about $140 stateside. Have you gotten my transmission from Autoland yet? If not, please get it put together.

Time to close out as I hear a chopper coming. If I miss this one it will be another three days before it gets mailed.

Keep the pound cake coming. Sure was good, and Kool-Aid.

All my love,

George

SERGEANT CHARLIE B. DICKEY *of Washington served with the U.S. Army, 1st Air Cavalry Division assigned to 1st Battalion 77th Artillery, attached to Charlie Company 2nd to the 5th Cavalry as a member of a Forward Observation Team involved in numerous search and destroy missions in and around Tay Nihn, III Corp. He was awarded the Air Medal, two Army Commendation Medals for Valor, two Purple Hearts, Vietnamese Cross of Gallantry, and the Silver Star for action on October 6, 1969. He was discharged in December of 1971.*

22 August 1969

My Very Dearest Wife,

It looks like for a change I might have the time to write a long letter. I'm still out in the jungle west of Phoc Vinh but my platoon will not be moving very far today. So I have the time to write you a decent letter.

In one of your letters you asked me just what my day was like. We get up around six A.M., eat, gather our stuff, and prepare to move out by seven. Our daily missions are sent by radio. Because I am in the F.O. party, I'm part of the morning briefing, so I know where we are going, which for me is pretty important as I need to know in case I need to call for Artillery or Cobra gunships. My job requires that I know where we are all times.

At about 10 A.M. we take a break, maybe 20–30 minutes. Now I drink my first water of the day. (I still make coffee in the morning.) Again we move out. Our usual mission is look for the NVA, we search for trails, bunkers, mortar, or rocket pits. Sometimes we find ammo or food caches, which we destroy.

How thick the jungle is determines how far and fast we move. If we think the NVA are in the area, we are extremely cautious, we trade time for distance. But always the days are hot, very hot. And most times the moves are very tiring. Lunch at noon, 30–45 minutes, and then we move again. We set up for the night around five

P.M. This consists of setting up a perimeter and everyone helps to dig a foxhole for the night. In my F.O. party there are three of us who take turns digging.

The Infantry guys set out trip flares and claymore mines. I call in artillery around the Night Defensive Position or NDP. We eat and as the sun goes down early we try to catch as much sleep as possible. Everyone pulls a two-hour watch at night. In my case I am in the middle of the NDP so I use the radio to check each major point around the perimeter every 15 minutes. If you pull radio watch at the beginning or the end of the night you can almost get a full night sleep. If not you have your sleep interrupted. All of us are tired.

There are times we encounter the enemy. I think the worst experience so far was outside LZ Ike on July 21. The night of the 20th a company of NVA hit us. We were digging in on a trail junction and they walked right in on us. The fight lasted about five hours. All night there were shots and explosions around us, some by us others by the NVA. The morning of the 21st we were mortared very heavily for about 30 minutes. Later on that morning I was walking up front with the point guys and we walked into a large ambush. As you can see I'm all right.

The tracker right in front of me was killed and there were many wounded. But the NVA broke contact and fled when I called in artillery and gunships.

I probably shouldn't tell you but I want you to know that there is a War over here. Men are being hurt and killed every day. Don't think this is just an adventure or having fun. This is hell. Besides killing and maybe being killed there are many other things that make life almost unbearable. Leeches that suck our blood, insects of all kinds, snakes, spiders (you KNOW how I feel about those). The heat, the rain and mud. The long marches with heavy pack, going two or three weeks without a bath, wearing the same clothes for weeks at a time, not having a place to sit down or even lie down except in six inches of mud.

Now my wife don't get me wrong, I am not complaining. It is my wish to be here doing my job. I know that any second might be my last. Yet I go willingly because there is a job I can do better than anyone else and I must do that job.

If the Lord decides He wants me with Him, I want you to know that I go into battle with a clear conscience and a very satisfied mind. You my Dear wife have played the biggest role in my life. If something should happen to me always remember that I have loved you above all.

Your loving Husband,
Charlie

*A typical day in the life of a nurse in South Vietnam is described by five Red Cross "clubmobile" workers with the "Big Red One" (1st Infantry Division):* JOYCE BRADY *of Harrisburg, Pennsylvania;* MARY CHERNEY *of Milwaukee, Wisconsin;* MIDGE PATTY *of Maryville, Tennessee;* LIZ MILLER *of Atlanta, Georgia; and* SANDY MONTGOMERY *of Chattanooga, Tennessee.*

March 30, 1966

A day in Vietnam is awaking at 6:00 in the morning to quiet, cool winds . . . walking from our tent to our powder-pink shower house . . . brushing our teeth out of a canteen . . . ironing our uniforms . . . sewing on the patch of the "Big Red One" . . . putting on our uniforms . . . walking down the long, dusty path in the soft morning sunlight to the mess hall . . . eating breakfast of soft powdered eggs and C-rations . . . being greeted by the men . . . walking to our working tent which serves as our Recreation Center . . . having a staff meeting . . . serving refreshments to the men . . . playing a game of Ping-Pong with an 18-year-old man . . . having meetings with the Commanders . . . serving food in a chow line . . . talking to the men . . . laughing with the men . . . walking back to the Recreation Center while melting in the noon sun . . . waving at a truckload of men who pass us on the road . . .

Getting in a helicopter and flying to the forward brigades . . . meeting with the Commanders of these brigades . . . setting up schedules to meet with their men . . . touring the area in an open jeep . . . riding in a tank . . . riding in an APC . . . waving to the men . . . taking pictures so we can send them home . . . viewing an area where Charlie had been hit the night before . . . shaking our heads in disbelief . . . talking to the men . . . smiling . . . waving . . . returning to the 1st Infantry Division headquarters by helicopter . . . watching the gunner in the helicopter scanning the jungles below for any sign of Charlie . . . landing at the helipad . . . getting in a ¾ ton truck to pick up supplies . . . unpacking supplies and putting them in the proper place . . . drawing and making props for our next program . . . another staff meeting . . . hearing the favorite saying in Vietnam, "Sorry about that" . . . walking back to our No. 1 Doll House (the name the men gave our tent) . . . showering off the red dust which had accumulated on us during the course of the day . . . dressing in civilian clothes . . . eating supper in a different mess hall . . . roast beef, powdered mashed potatoes, corn pudding, bread and butter, Kool-Aid . . . talking to the men . . . discussing the temperature of the day, 125 degrees . . . laughing because we knew it had been hot . . . walking to the "outdoor movie" and admiring the caldron of color in the evening sunset . . . taking our weekly malaria pill . . . drenching ourselves with mosquito repellent . . . walking back to our tent . . . being challenged by the MP on guard . . . giving the password . . . walking down the dusty path armed with our flashlight . . . walking past the barbed wire . . . walking past our bunker hoping we'd never have to use it . . . walking to our patio that the men built for us as a surprise . . . talking with the girls . . . discussing the events of the day . . . watching in silence the flares being shot off in the distance . . . hearing the artillery firing . . . being thankful that it is outgoing fire instead of incoming . . . feeling secure because we are being protected by the finest group of men in the world . . . washing out our uniforms . . . laughing at our hardships . . . rolling our hair . . . walking to our "outdoor facility" one last time . . . spraying disinfectant all around our tent . . . checking our bed for snakes, scorpions, roaches, or any other nice things . . . getting into bed . . . tucking our mosquito netting around us . . . hearing the artillery firing in the distance but not listening to it . . . writing a letter home . . . sealing the letter . . . looking at the letter, knowing how much it will be appreciated by our families . . . thinking of home . . . saying good night to the other girls . . . turning off our flashlights and placing them under our pillows . . . turning over . . . being alone . . . alone to say our prayers . . . alone to think . . . to think of new ideas for our program . . . planning and formulating . . . planning activities for the next day and the next day and the next day . . . sleeping . . . dreaming of the day when our program will be fully operational so we can serve more men better . . . dreaming of the day when we will not be needed in Vietnam . . . dreaming of peace.

WO-1 RICHARD ELLIOT, *with the First Cavalry Division (Air), offers some glimpses into the life of a soldier out of combat with these excerpts from letters written to his father in Clearwater, Florida.*

April 1966

We moved, and now we are about 40 miles north of Plei-Ku.

We are next to a river, though, and we go swimming and bathing at every chance. The native women also go there, but they stay a little upstream. The bad part is we will probably only stay here a few days if we don't find any Cong.

We will probably stay out in the field until the middle of May. I've forgotten what it is like to even sleep on a cot. . . .

. . . We got in from the field Monday, after 24 days. We may go back out in about a week. First night in, we all went to the club to blow off steam. There was a party in one of the guys' tents. All in all it was a pretty relaxing night.

I started correspondence courses. I'm going to take Algebra I and II, and trigonometry. Then start on college credits. Much fun!

Well, I'm back in the field for a few days, then back to An Khe. Thank goodness. The bugs here are terrible. . . .

. . . This is sure pretty country up north here. Our camp is by a river, and some of the boys were panning gold from it. . . .

June 1966

We are here on the coast. It isn't too bad. We park our ships right on the beach at night, and the cool ocean breezes keep all the bugs away. . . .

It is really pretty country down here. Mountains, green slopes, palm trees, beautiful beaches. There would be a lot of promise for this country if there wasn't a war, and if the people weren't so lousy. Oh, well! . . .

July 1966

. . . Puss Puss [his cat] died. I made the mistake of leaving him with a friend when we went into the field. Oh well, I'll just find another pet.

I got two more cats. These are even smaller than Puss Puss was when I got her. All they do is eat and sleep. Well, anyway, they are cute and I'm softhearted. . . .

AIRMAN, FIRST CLASS FRANK PILSON *was born and raised in Springfield, Delaware County, Pennsylvania, and served in the Air Force with Air Force Security on search and destroy missions while in Vietnam from April 28, 1966, to April 25, 1967. His honors include the Air Force Good Conduct Ribbon, Presidential Unit Citation, and National Defense Service Medal.*

*Airman Pilson wrote the following undated letter home to his mother, Anne Pilson, in Springfield, Pennsylvania.*

*Airman First Class Frank Pilson*
*shown guarding fuel oil for F-4C aircraft*
*(photo by USAF photographer)*

Dear Mom,

Well today started out as a nice quiet day but at about 1300 hours everything broke loose. They woke us up and called us down to work, the whole 12 A.P. Sqd, were told that a VIP was coming in.

90

I guess you know that the President and his party were due at Cam Ranh Bay. We were issued weapons (M-16), I was in the Honor guard, right up front, second from the left, so I saw everything. I guess I should start from the beginning. The President arrived in AF1 on time, 1630 he got off AF1. He and Westmoreland reviewed the troops—Army, Navy, Marines—and the 12 AP sqd., he went right by me, not more that 15 feet away. He looked tired and worn-out—his is not an easy job. He gave a speech—he told us we were doing a great job and all Americans are with us. It was a short speech and then he left. They picked 40 of the AP to eat dinner with him, guess who one of the 40 were—me! The President came in and the press were all around asking questions and writing down everything he did, said, and ate.

I do not even know what he had, we had a band playing "Yellow Rose of Texas." The President then gave a short speech telling us how proud he was of us and that all the Americans were behind us. They would never abandon us or Vietnam. I sure felt proud to be an American Fighting Man and Air Policeman. It is not often we see our commander-in-chief, but after 37 months, today was worth waiting for.

He left and took a tour of the base and left at about 1300 on AF1. I never would have seen LBJ in the states, I had to come to Vietnam to see him. Maybe you will see it on the news and see what the country does really look like. Send me information about it— did you see me?

So now everything is back to normal, I really felt proud that he came to see us. I hope peace comes to VN and we can leave this a free country. I know why I am over here, so now to work and then sleep.

Today was a day to remember, I am proud to be an American.

Love,
Frank

MRS. ACHSA JANE REEDER, *an American Red Cross worker, writes of some of her experiences in serving American soldiers in South Vietnam.*

Dear Hearts at Home . . .

How wonderful it would be to sit and talk with each of you this Christmas time. However, this is the only instrument at hand with which to achieve contact, so it must suffice.

The tape recorder upstairs is playing some marvelous music of the Mormon Tabernacle choir, the one downstairs has some cat on a bugle . . . all very fitting background for writing.

My assignment to Vietnam came as sort of a birthday present. Suddenly there was a need for what I could do, case work and book-keeping. At first it was just to finish the tour which ends 7 January. . . . As I boarded the plane it was suggested that I was of course going to extend? . . .

The trip down was smooth and uneventful, other than having as a seat partner the new [Red Cross] Director of Operations for the area. He was the VIP on the flight and took me along into the protocol lounges which made it most pleasant indeed because it was very warm in Okinawa and the Philippines. Saigon was our destination and it fascinated me. In many ways it was much like Taiwan, but also quite different. My favorite sport during the week I spent awaiting orders for Nha Trang was sitting in the open-air bar of the Continental Palace Hotel watching the traffic. . . .

I spent the first few days delighted with Saigon and the fascinating marketplace that was straight out of Ali Baba or the Thief of Bagdad, merchants squatting by their brass and porcelain ware, beggars picking at your clothes, so many of them of all ages and stages.

The day finally arrived and we climbed aboard a C-123, cargo-type plane with bucket seats, you sit in a sort of sling. The trip was short and smooth. The field director greeted us effusively and I was escorted to my "villa." Anything under a roof is called a villa here. I live with the nurses in the villa, my roomie is the [Red Cross] hospital field directress.

I interrupt to say we just had news of the bombing of the Metropole Hotel in Saigon, a dreadful thing. We had gone several months with comparatively few incidents of that nature, but I suppose we can expect more for a time now. Charlie usually cuts up more during monsoon and holiday time.

My last trip to Saigon was not very successful and the trip home was hairy to say the least. The plane lost an engine and we were strapped in for crash landing . . . crash lights blazing. I was thinking, I wonder if this is how I am destined to go, and worrying about the young courier next to me who had just told me about the new baby he had never seen. I was quite surprised at how calm I remained, just waiting and praying it would be quick. But being geared for the performance of my life I couldn't very well go on without an audience . . . so we made it.

We are now in the throes of Operation Santa Claus. Today 15,000 pounds of cookies arrived. Don't send any more till Easter please. One outfit parachuted down nearly a ton of goodies to the fellows in the jungle. I believe every man of them will have a gift no matter where he is, from a stranger who is a friend, and a letter from a child.

I am about to write the newspaper in Indianapolis, all the packages were from that area. We spent all day recording gifts and getting out acknowledgments so they won't feel their efforts were in vain. Most of ours will go to the sick and wounded in the Army hospital here.

We don't often get to deliver good news, you know, but occasionally people have first babies, and this was one of those times. We had a PIO man here and took turns going out with him for photos. The day came when I was allowed to deliver the message. The Marine was aboard a ship but in the stream. There didn't seem to be anything available, and about that time it began to rain. As we walked into a shed I spied a corporal whose picture we had taken on a previous visit. To our good fortune he turned out to be in charge of the Light Amphibious Resupply Craft, that are like long-bodied trucks that drive in and over the sea.

We actually found our lad . . . standing there directing cargo loading, and it was the ideal situation. He had been pacing the deck because the baby was due and his mail hadn't caught up with him. It was his first baby, he wanted a girl and he got a girl, and all was fine. The picture we got of that boy was something beautiful in the way of a smile. It's the Christmas miracle all over again and to have been a part in it renews your strength too. . . .

Fondly,
Achsa Jane

COLONEL CHESTER B. MCCOID II *spent more than 55 months in Vietnam from June 1966 until 1973. According to his son-in-law, John (Jack) Kennedy, Colonel McCoid was the last combat soldier to leave the city of Da Nang on March 29, 1973.*

*A veteran of World War II and Korea, Colonel McCoid went to Vietnam in June 1966 as Deputy Brigade Commander of the 101st Airborne Division and served more than eight major assignments in Vietnam until his departure on March 29, 1973, including negotiating directly with the NVA concerning the logistics of releasing prisoners of war. He was most proud of the Combat Infantry Badge, which he won three times—one of only 290 in U.S. history to do so. He passed away in January 2000 and was buried with full military honors.*

*He wrote the following letters home to his wife, Dorothy.*

*Colonel Chester B. McCoid II, deputy commander of the 101st Airborne Division, and his son, Chester B. McCoid III, who was with the 1st Cavalry Division (Airmobile), Vietnam, Christmas 1966 (U.S. Army Photograph)*

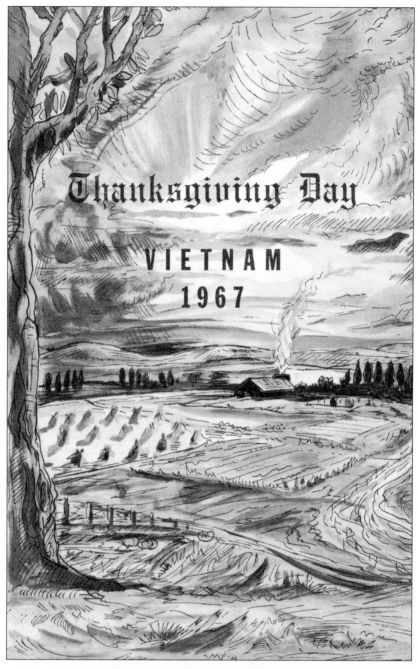

*Menu for the troops' Thanksgiving Day dinner, 1967.*
*Col. Chester McCoid wrote a letter home on the back.*

# THANKSGIVING DAY DINNER

Shrimp Cocktail

Crackers

Roast Turkey

Turkey Gravy      Cornbread Dressing      Cranberry Sauce

Mashed Potatoes      Glazed Sweet Potatoes

Buttered Mixed Vegetable

Assorted Crisp Relishes

Hot Rolls      Butter      Fruit Cake      Mincemeat Pie

Pumpkin Pie w/Whipped Topping

Assorted Nuts      Assorted Candy      Assorted Fresh Fruits

Tea w/Lemon      Milk

Thanksgiving Day —

As you can see, the troops who can get a hot meal will do very well this year. Unfortunately, many will not because of the heavy action throughout II Corps (IFFORCEV's domain).

Since Nha Trang is far from the scene of major action, my senior NCO — a fine, tough sergeant major — took me to dinner at the enlisted mess. It was very enjoyable.

Noted that Bill Ver Hey had been picked up as a 5 percenter for promotion to colonel, which is very good going indeed! Also noted that our old friend (with the drinking wife) Chaplain Skelton had been selected. As you say, many bright young fellows are sure to feel that they are on their way. In Kingston's case it will be well deserved for he is an unusually fine fighting officer

All my love
Cheeter

21 August 1966
Tuy Hoa, South Vietnam

Dearest Dorothy:

Last evening I called Mackey at An Khe. He is not in trouble; has not been promoted; claims to have written you on 16 August, after delay during which he was on duty in Saigon. The telephone was rather poor so I cannot report any lengthy conversations with him; however, I did instruct him to write you once a week in future.

Today General Westmoreland visited the brigade and brought with him Mr. Chet Huntley of NBC-TV. I briefed the latter while General Pearson closeted with the former. Huntley is rather heavier and older looking in real life than on television. Only his voice seemed exactly the same.

Yesterday I went on a liaison visit to the command post of the 1st Marine Division at Chu Lai. We found them living in near-splendor, complete with air-conditioned offices and flush plumbing. They are doing their usual effective job, albeit at much greater cost than we require, for we live relatively primitive lives in the heat and sand. Actually they did have a sign along the main road at Chu Lai which amused me; it read: "Los Angeles, 9875 miles ahead, keep in the right lane."

Several days ago your letter mentioned that Haggis had wet on the new door. I assume that it is a new storm door off the kitchen; if so please let me know just which windows have been provided for. Perhaps we should have the rest done as well? In any case I am anxious to keep the house in as good condition as is possible for it represents our only stable investment. Be sure that you put a second coat of paint on the window sash which I puttied and on the repair job on the big window in the basement. Additionally, pull out each of the termite inspection stakes every now and then and check for signs of infestation.

Recently I have been trying to locate items of local manufacture which might be useful and interesting for our living room. So far nothing worthwhile has turned up. As you know I have always sought to locate a bell for my Aunt May in any new country in which I visit. Even something as simple as a bell is difficult to find. The locals use bells for signals such as curfew, but their bells are sections of railroad rail which are clanged with a hammer or rod of iron. The Buddhists use gongs; however, Tuy Hoa is a center of Roman Catholicism, so we don't see saffron robes in the streets here. In fact there is no pagoda locally although there are several shrines to Buddha around the district. General Dayan and I visited a couple of them during his visit here. The odor of the joss sticks was quite strong, for a number were smoldering before the central figure of the seated god in each case.

The rice harvest has begun at Phan Rang, while some of the fields here are beginning to ripen. One of our main functions is to protect the farmers as they take in their grain. We do so by fighting the Viet Cong in the hills to the north and west. If we were not here, the valley would be a waste of land; as it is they expect to process up to 40,000 metric tons by the end of the year. This will be more than sufficient to feed the local population, so some will be available for shipment to Saigon. All in all it represents a potential saving for the U.S. taxpayer, for we have to pay for every pound of rice which must be imported into this land to feed the population. The enemy here is the difficult-to-identify local guerrilla. He wears the usual black, coolie pajamas and a broad peaked hat of painted palm leaves. Unless you sight him with his weapon, or unless he is in a restricted zone, he cannot be engaged by fire. As I indicated in an earlier letter, he is the sneak saboteur who snipes, throws grenades, plants mines, and commits atrocities. So we are losing a few casualties each day, and we can't force the little bastards to fight. Once in a while we trap a party of several and then rub them out. Individually they aren't worth much; fighting from ambush they manage to give a fair account of themselves. Most are equipped with German weapons which were captured during the Second World War by the Russians and since sent here for use against us. It is novel to see some of the same weapons one saw in battle over 20 years ago. Of course they do use Chinese, Czech, Russian, and North Vietnamese items; and they also use our weapons which they have captured from the Army of South Vietnam. The regulars of North Vietnam are quite conventional and easy to identify for they use only weapons of communist origin and wear uniforms which are simple but recognizable.

Our troops much prefer fighting the guerrillas for they do not fight to the end and are easier to defeat in the long run.

The people who are really proving their worth out here are the veterans of the two earlier wars. Although some of the NCOs are in or nearing their fifties (as is First Sergeant Sabolovsky, whom I visited a couple of days ago), they are more daring and devoted to duty than the 20-year-olds. Unfortunately they are the men whose loss we can ill afford and yet we lose them. I found that some of the younger officers are very fine, but a few seem to avoid much real action by a display of fancy footwork. I intend seeing that all are tested fully before this is over, as there are too many prima donnas around who are more concerned with making general than killing the VC. I am also convinced that the rear area is overrun with far more personnel than are needed to support this war with a real degree of effectiveness. Actually only about one man in three in this brigade really kills the foe, which the average for the theater is perhaps one man in eight. All the rest are sock counters and paper pushers, pill rollers and legal clerks.

Well, darling, I must be off.

All of my love to you all,
Chester

12 August 1966
Tuy Hoa, South Vietnam

Dearest Dorothy:

Several days have passed since last writing you, due mainly to our pursuing a North Vietnamese Army Artillery Battalion. Thus far we have them on the run; we have killed quite a number, captured several and taken a lot of matériel. An incident of some little interest was capturing a 100 bed field hospital, without its patients— some of whom we are now scooping up.

The hospital was made entirely of native materials, including brush, bamboo, living trees, and palmetto leaves—the latter for roofing and siding. Just before burning it, so that the enemy cannot use it in the future, the troops were destroying cooking pots. I looked at them carefully and found many to be of cast brass. I rescued two that were least badly damaged and am now having them brazed in Tuy Hoa. They are handsomely cast; are some 20 inches across the middle and are 102 inches high. In cross-section they look about as follows:

The mouth of the vessel is 163 inches wide; as you can see there are two small loops by which the pot can be suspended over a fire. Unfortunately, they have had a pick driven through them—thus the necessity of the repairs. If one can be thankful it is because only the bottoms have been holed, so the brazing will be simple. Once I get mine back I will have it cleaned up and posted to you. Actually it should arrive in time for your anniversary gift! I should say in passing that it must weigh 15 pounds or more.

This campaign is far from finished. We will need many more troops before we are through out here. Our troops are markedly superior to the enemy in action, but it is hard to bring them to bay. The local forces are tired, and not really a match for the troops from the north, all of whom are regulars. However, the South Vietnamese troops could handle the Viet Cong, most of whom are really only good for laying mines, sniping, and setting booby traps. We have no trouble pounding the VC when we can catch up with them—they wisely pull out if they can. Most of our officers and NCOs have a grudging admiration for the courage and steadfastness of the North Vietnamese, but only active dislike for the Viet Cong, who seem to specialize in acts of terror against the defenseless. Just two days ago they tortured a 17-year-old girl who was to marry a government soldier. They smashed her face with rifle butts and tore off part of her scalp, then left her dying in the road (where she was found too late to save). Needless to say, not much mercy is left in anyone's heart after an atrocity like that.

This evening there is a brisk breeze blowing off the mountains to the west; the temperature is down to about 80 degrees, consequently we are much more comfortable than is usual. Too bad we could not hope for cooler weather with the lengthening year and shortening days. But that is not to be, for these are the tropics. The heat and humidity are no worse than Okinawa (or Georgia) in midsummer—on the other hand there is no winter season of sharper temperatures. Actually this breeze appears to be a distant offshoot of the typhoon conditions on the China coast to the north. Thus far the sand hasn't started to blow, a condition which can be most miserable. One additional benefit is the absence of insects in really large numbers at the moment. Your particular enemies, the mosquitoes, are not to be seen or heard. We do sleep under nets which are fully effective if tucked in carefully. However, the hum of 20 or 30 hungry lady mosquitoes is a rather unsatisfactory lullaby, net or no.

The enemy matériel we have taken so far is from all over the communist world, although China and the Soviet Union seem to be providing the bulk of it. We find ammunition from Poland and Czechoslovakia, medicines (particularly penicillin) from Bulgaria, gasoline lanterns from East Germany, wound dressings from Romania, and toothpaste from North Vietnam. Much of it is in rather good condition despite having been carried hundreds of miles on coolies' backs along jungle trails. We find that we cannot allow our troops to abandon any metal container larger than a C-ration can in the field, for the enemy will find some use for it. An example of their resourcefulness was seen in their hospital. Obviously many of their wounded were, or once were, unable to walk. For urinals they had cut lengths of bamboo about 24 inches long and about two inches across. By cutting out all of the interstices or insides of the joints they would hold about a quart. Ergo a urinal!! I don't think they are well enough fed to need bed pans; at least, we didn't see any. As far as food was concerned we found that they had recently butchered a pig there and that they had some salt, rice, and a stock of peas of miniature size. They also had some sweet corn that was pathetically underdeveloped. About the only food that was clearly hospital fare was some tinned milk which was from Hanoi.

I don't want to run out of things to write about so will now bring this letter to a close. Please give my love to Maureen, Scott, Naomi, and Haggis.

Love,

Chester

P.S. We have been undergoing an I.G. inspection. One of the inspectors is Major Puckett, who was a Captain-Aviator in the 2/503–173; he sends his best to you.

C

SP-5 WILLIAM M. (MIKE) KEVILLE *of Wheaton, Illinois, spent three years with the Army in Germany before his assignment to Vietnam. The letters he wrote while a company clerk with the 27th Maintenance Battalion of the 1st Cavalry Division reveal a flair for irony and wry humor.*

Thursday P.M.

Nov. 4th, 1965

Dear Folks,

. . . Last night, between 10:30 and midnight, I finally contributed directly to the war effort. Fifty yards behind us is an 81mm mortar platoon (the one that keeps us awake all through the night), and over the course of the weeks we've become quite friendly with them; i.e., we slip them hot food and beer; they slip us wild bananas captured from some village, etc. Yesterday a few of them came over and invited myself and one Ed Doolittle—a jester from Connecticut—to get in on the action. That night, they showed us how the things are set up, how they get their coordinates, and all that mathematical garbage, plus how to fuse the rounds, etc. They had two fire missions (harassing fire in case Charlie lurks in the nearby glen) and let Ed and me drop six rounds apiece down the tube. The command "Prepare to fire," then "Hang it" (insert the projectile into the tube), and "Fire," whereupon you drop the thing, duck down as if tying your shoelace, open your mouth and holler—lest your eardrums become ruptured—and KA-POW . . . off she goes. Some 20 seconds later comes the explosion, a thousand or two yards up front. What a blast! I wonder if we killed any Cong . . . probably not, and—truthfully, in a way—I hope not. Anyway, those guys are sure proud of what they're doing, and they love to show people all about it. I'm afraid I'd never hack it though: too much math! We have an open invitation to go fire any time they have a mission, and to show our appreciation, we—ah—"obtained" 14 air-mattresses for them, as they sleep on the ground. . . .

After last night's feeling of *doing* something, it was back to the dull, routine around here today. Well, *almost* dull, but that can wait! You know, the hardest part of all this is the feeling of sitting around on our ferns, doing nothing, while all around us the war rages. Some of our guys, the 1/9 Cavalry Squadron got pretty well chewed up over Plei Me, but are now returning the favors. To mar an otherwise drowsy afternoon, a "Huey" [aircraft] mysteriously blew up near An Khe: all aboard killed. We saw them trucking-in part of the wreckage—wasn't much left. Enough of that garbage, because here's the high spot of the day:

After weeks of wondering "will it?" "or won't it?" (only the weatherman knows for sure)—my sleeping bag and liner finally dried out. Get it? Completely, deliciously dried-out. A Posturepedic should be so beloved! Well, to shed the thing of some of the odor that tends to accumulate, I lovingly placed both the sleeping bag and poncho liner (serves as a pillow) on top of the tent to bask in the broiling sun. Just *knowing* that my "portable rack" was going to be fresh as a daisy for tonight, I accepted the First Sergeant's offer to hop in the jeep and "go look for some lumber." Ah, peace at last! We roamed the expanse of that ultramodern thruway known quaintly as the Peripheral Boundary, reveling in the cool breeze of a missing windshield at 35 miles per hour, when, about 11 miles from the compound, there did ensue the most HELLACIOUS downpour ever witnessed by civilized man! "Noooooooo Sweat-e-da, though, Pussycat . . . my PALS will bring in my sleeping bag if it rains back there!" Yeah. Uh-huh. My pals. Returning to the compound, thoroughly soaked, but in good spirits because we could towel-down and spend an evening in a dry, warm sack, my 20/400 eyes did perceive a *most* distressing sight: there (as you by now know) in all its radiant glory, as soggy as a year-old Cornflake in a cesspool, was the item in question. Tonight I will sleep fully clothed on a damp bunk; tonight I will softly curse my pals; tonight I will become a convert to sleeping in dry, *stinky* sleeping bags. Ah, yes, tonight will be Hell. *Tomorrow,* I begin the drying process all over. . . .

Love,

Mike

March 8th, 1966

(121 days left)

Dear Folks,

Got the package. Boy, what goodies. . . . You might know it, but the night before [the film] arrived, we had the most beautiful sunset ever . . . right behind Hon-Cong it was, and contained every color imaginable. To illustrate just how great it was, most of the Company stood for at least 15 minutes staring at it . . . and *that* takes something special for these unartistic hunks to get worked up about! The sky was a brilliant blue, with wisps of luminous clouds way up there, and the horizon was a wash of blues, greens, yellow, orange, etc., but the crowning touch was the three distinct shafts of bright red-orange that shot up from the horizon. And me with no color film! I gnashed my teeth the rest of the night. What did we have *last* night? You guessed it: boiling storm clouds. I almost staged a demonstration! . . .

Love,

Mike

LIEUTENANT COLONEL MARIANNE REYNOLDS *wrote the follow-ing letter home to her parents in Monterey Park, California. Reynolds had just arrived in-country the month before as a civilian after grad-uating from college and was stationed at Dong Tam and then Can Tho with the U.S. Army Special Services. Lieutenant Reynolds joined the military upon her return to the United States and served over 20 years as a public affairs officer. She came into the military as First Lieu-tenant on a direct commission in 1975.*

Monday, Sept. 25, 1967

Hi,

Got a kick out of this card as I spent six hours this morning waiting for a chopper back to Dong Tam from Saigon (sigh). Finally got a ride from Navy Special Forces—the guys are so great to us, help us at every turn, and makes me so happy and proud I'm an American girl [smiley face].

Opening of club at Long Binh very nice. My escort for the day real sweet boy from St. Joseph, Kansas! Knew of Wathena (sp?) too. Got to stop for two hour layover at Bearcat on way up. Visited with Mac and ate lunch.

Rode up yesterday on a large plane called a Caraboo [drew photo of plane]. A real experience as they are hit so often you must climb at about 90 degree angle at take-off and dive on landing to avoid ground fire. I think I'd like to stick to the choppers!!

Couldn't believe it yesterday but my salary for one month here was $746.62. Had much taken out for Fed. Inc. tax & to repay $300 loan but eh gods I'll owe my soul to Uncle Sam at Income Tax time if I keep making this much each month! [frowny face]

Have the orphans coming down this Saturday from My Tho, and Father Brinkman and I arranged for the pilots from Soc Tran to fly up and take the kids for a chopper ride. Will be the event of their lives, I'm sure, and I'm really excited for them.

Carlotta got her letter back she sent to David the day before he died. Sort of sad as she had enclosed a St. Christopher medal which we got while in Saigon. I'm sad and yet thankful to God, I was made to keep myself detached from certain things—Paivika showed me I had this in me. Things get tight now & then emotionally but always, almost miraculously, something or someone comes by and gets me back on the right track again.

Love my work, drains me but I'm keeping healthy. I've really got a trim bod—118 lbs.—I feel great & am eating good. Meeting wonderful friends, and learning so many new things to add to my philosophy on life. Will write soon,

Love ya,<br>Marianne

[The card read: "Dear Folks—Now that I am in Vietnam, I know you miss me as much as I'm missing you. But there is one good thing: I have your picture and letters (shows a cartoon G.I. writing). Turn card to read: AND YOU HAVE THE KEYS TO THE CAR."]

CAPTAIN BOBBIE (MACLEAN) FRY *arrived in Vietnam in March 1967 and served as captain in the Army Nurse Corps. Her honors include the Army Presidential Unit Citation. Captain Fry wrote the following letter to her parents, Ralph and Carol Ann MacLean, in South Portland, Maine.*

*Sp5 Jackie Hughes and Captain Bobbie MacLean Fry (R), between casualties in 7th Surgery pre-op, January 23, 1968. Bobbie Fry left Vietnam one month later. (Photo by Capt. Leeanna Clutter A.N.C., their O.R. nurse.)*

8 Mar. 67

Dear Mom and Dad,

Hope all is well at home. Found out today I'll be staying at the 7th Surg. which is moving to Xuan Loc. The staff should go around the first of April to get ready for casualties. In the interim we're all being assigned to other hospitals in the area TDY, temporary duty. I'll be here at the 12th Evac for a few more days then go to the 24th Evac at Long Binh. Each ward here is a separate Quonset hut named for a state, but I haven't found Maine yet, probably never will. A lot of the patients are ambulatory which is so good to see as so many others are amputees. There is also a VC patient here.

The CO of the 7th Surg. took another nurse and myself into the village of Cu Chi. Got a little lamp for 290 piasters, about $2.50. The Vietnamese children surrounded our jeep to get a good look. They're so cute. Our base camp at Cu Chi has an odor I don't think I'll ever forget. It's a combination of red clay, tar, oil, and heat, lots of heat! I'm sleeping in a storeroom with another nurse, but really haven't slept all that much. I was warned that this place gets noisy at night when the guns start firing but wasn't prepared to have my bed shake. The rats are also active at night and have gotten into my things. In addition we have two dogs, Cocoa and Raven, and a mynah bird named Joe.

I thought the social life in the states was great but it's even better here. The troops are always sending jeeps over to transport us to their parties and I've met a lot of nice people so far. How strange to be laughing, drinking, and dancing with gunfire in the background—it's so crazy.

Will write more later.

Love,
Bobbie

*Captain Fry wrote the following letter to her parents while she was with the 7th Surgery at Black Horse Base Camp, 11th Armored Cavalry.*

21 May 67

Dear Mom and Dad,

Today we had another mass cal [casualty]. It helps that I can talk to you about it. Know it upsets you, too, am sorry. We filled up pre-op right away with the severely wounded and holding ward with the less serious. But it was the last two choppers crammed with bodies that I hope I can forget someday. They were lining them up out in front of the hosp. side by side waiting for graves registration to take them away. My heart aches for their buddies who saw them being loaded off the chopper.

I worked in post-op tonight and found out it was a convoy that was attacked. My patients saw what they thought were ARVN soldiers standing by the side of the road but when they came upon them, they opened fire. They said the VC were crawling everywhere. That's the way it is over here. You just don't know who or where your enemies are. We lost one in the OR but the rest are doing okay.

But would you believe after what they went through we had two red alerts tonight. Put mattresses on those we couldn't move and got the others on the floor under the beds. No peace. No sleep.

Know you'll remember all these men in your prayers.

Love and God bless,

Bobbie

*In the following letter to her parents, Captain MacLean Fry refers to a wounded baby named Peaches who was operated on by the commanding officer of the 7th Surgery. He later adopted her.*

24 Sept. 67

Dear Mom and Dad,

Hope everything's fine in Maine. Sure miss you guys. Thanks for your offer to send Peaches some things but she's leaving us in a couple of days. She got her passport and is heading for California. She's gotten fat and happy and her hand is healing well. We've all become so attached to her and will miss her dearly when she's gone. She's certainly been a morale booster for the patients too, but has a real good opportunity at life now.

Aside from being a med-surg and peds hospital, 7th Surg. can now add obstetrics. The chopper landed yesterday with a pregnant Vietnamese woman, her husband, and mother-in-law. She was ready to deliver except that a little arm was already presenting. We did a

C-section and mama and baby girl are doing just fine. Papa has strung up his hammock in front of the hospital. We'll probably evac. them to a Vietnamese hosp. in a couple of days.

Word has it that the female nurses here may be reassigned to an Evac hosp. All the replacements have been male lately. Hope it's not true. I don't want to leave this place, actually love this old mud hole and the people I'm with. I'm as safe here as anywhere.

Had a nice surprise. Was leafing through the Sears catalog on the ward and was voicing how much I would love to have a bike. Lo and behold a few days later my dear corpsmen presented me with a bike, freshly painted OD Green. Told me to ride it on the back roads and avoid the MPs. Will send a picture. These guys are the greatest.

Work is quiet this week so we're back on an eight-hour shift—always subject to change at a moment's notice.

Take care of yourselves.

Love and God bless,
Bobbie

*Captain Bobbie Maclean Fry with her "new" bike, September 1967
(photo by Capt. Leeanna Clutter A.N.C.)*

CHAPLAIN BILL LIBBY *wrote home to his wife, Amelia, who was living in Dumas, Texas, and his parents, who saved almost all of his letters home. They were written between December 1, 1967 and November 15, 1968, while Bill served with the 101st Division Artillery as chaplain. Originally stationed at Bien Hoa Air Force Base as the Base Camp for 101st Airborne Division, he moved regularly with the units and soldiers of the brigade to various fire bases and combat areas, serving at a number of well-known fire bases, including Bastogne, Birmingham, and Veghel. Chaplain Libby was awarded the Vietnam Service Ribbon, an Air Medal, and two Bronze Stars.*

January 1968

Dear Babe,

Life goes on—many changes in plans. I have been traveling considerably the last few days. Seen a lot of country, much of it empty of people.

Sunday flew to Song Be near Cambodian border. We (U.S.) moved in and built a camp on top of a bamboo plantation. The ground is red silt, very loose, and every step raises a cloud of dust. Speed limits there are five mph to help the problem. But from miles away you can see the cloud of dust.

Monday morning I drove to Cu Chi on business—spent most of the day. On the way back Ben and I passed a broken down car which turned out to be an ambulance. I noticed a woman lying in the grass on the side of the road. She was having a baby. We stopped for a moment to make sure she was O.K., then went back down the road to get an MP who was guarding a bridge. He called a chopper in to take her to the hospital. Two old ladies took the baby to a creek and washed him off while another rolled the afterbirth in a newspaper and threw it in the bushes. At last the chopper came and we sent her away with the baby. Number 1 excitement of the day.

Ben and I had also seen straw mats we wanted in some little shops. Stopped a man on a bike and bought two from him—floor mats with strips dyed in at each end—$3.00 each—but they help keep the dust down.

Bien Hoa has been expecting attack now for some time but nothing yet. North of us yesterday one of our infantry battalions got hit badly—fighting all day long.

Must run.

Love,

Bill

*Chaplain Libby wrote the following letter to his mother and father-in-law, the Reverend and Mrs. William F. Dunkle, Jr., of Wilmette, Illinois.*

Fri., 16 Feb. (68)

Dear Folks—

A pleasant Friday morning—cool and quiet, as there aren't normally any guns at this hour. Weather has been nice ever since we came—monsoon had just ended then in this area. Now the dry season is with us—no rain since 4 Dec.—the heat rises about 10 to 1030 each day and stays very bad until 1600. The only bad thing is the constant dust in the air, and any sort of breeze kicks up more.

Have heard on the news that 10,000 more are coming over pretty quick here. Am beginning to feel that the need to bring more right now exists only because those here are not being adequately used—we have established something of a bureaucracy here and thousands of troops are involved in administrative office jobs with more thousands necessary to guard them. Much of the strategy in this area seems to be to sit in our little defended base camps and wait for the VC, with very little actual going and looking. There is so much frustration among our experienced people here. They feel some measure of being held back, of hesitancy, of satisfaction with merely "holding the line" with no vigorous action. No, I'm not becoming nor do I desire to become a tactician. But I'm beginning to see some of the reasons for the frustration with Viet Nam.

Within three weeks it is expected that the 101 will be on the DMZ in the general area Quang Tri to Khe Sanh. However, this depends on the situation here and there, and transportation.

You wanted to know a little of my activities. It is centered in two areas, I think. Group services and personal contacts. When the artillery firing batteries are in the fire bases, I go there for services normally with a priest so that we can offer both services. These services are usually small—I've had as few as three and as many as 40, but 20–25 is normal. When our batteries are in their base camps, three of them are not within walking distance of chapels, so I try to have a service every other week on a weekday. I take the priest with me, and again have the two services. Our units are very good about this—if there are no fire missions going on, they just shut down for services so that those who want to go will feel completely free. So I have 3–5 services weekly but only one each Sunday. The Sunday service is in a Quonset Chapel at Bien Hoa. Some of the services are in EM clubs, some out in the open, some in barracks. One Sunday afternoon six of us including one RC [Roman Catholic] and one Gr Orth [Greek Orthodox] had two hour hymn sing in a bunker underground—not deep enough to stand in—you either had to lie flat or sit down—it was the sleeping bunker for two of the men— covered with timber and sandbags. Another time I had services in an underground chapel—a "lower room" with boxes for an altar. The cross on the wall was made of two branches and a coil of barbed wire—our own perimeter wire—the crown of thorns. Lighting was by lantern—quite a situation. Each time I have a service in the field I have Communion . . . I always have Communion by instinction—the cups are useless over here—and I always take the elements to the troops. It is difficult for them to move easily with steel helmet in the lap and rifles on the shoulder. But I do remind them that the reception of communion is their choice and they should nod to me if they do not want to receive, and each time there are several who do not. . . . Have knowingly given to RC's and Gr Orth in situations where they could not get to services of their own. To continue with my activities—each morning at 0715 we have a briefing and again at 1600. I am expected to be present for each. The morning is a ré-sumé of the tactical situation of the last 24 hours. And a forecast of things to come. The other meeting is more of information on gen-eral activities—to share with the rest of the staff general informa-tion. Some days I go out for the day just to spend time with the men—just talking individually and in small groups—pastoral calls, if you will. This is very important, I think, for it gives the troops time to talk about home, food, sex, etc. I also go to the hospital—we have two large ones 15 minutes away by jeep—but the road is safe only in daytime. Near the hospitals is a stockade—huge one in fact—and we have one man there. Once a week I try to get to a nearby Dominican convent in a village of RC refugees from N. Vietnam. They are quite anxious to have us visit them. Then there is some time for study, reading, etc., though not as much as I should. I get the Methodist magazines, including the *Religion in Life*, the *Nat Cath Reporter*, and beginning next month *Christian Century* and *Christianity Today*. The *Stars and Stripes*—noncommit-tal as it is—comes regularly, but in this area we have available *Time, Life, Post*, etc.

*Sat. morning*. Each day I try to get some exercise—volleyball, running, swimming, etc.—not always possible. In five minutes we are going on a Med Cap—Medical Civil Action Program—the doc-tor takes basic medical supplies to a local village for sick call—they teach basic health techniques like the value of clean hands and teeth. However, this is a continual business as the people don't stay with it.

*Sat. eve 17 Feb*. Am sitting at a picnic table under a parachute canopy—an outdoor club—nearby 10 men are playing basketball like "back on the block"—the goal is mounted on a telephone pole, sides are roughly marked off, and the court is a dirty rough road.

The Med Cap this morning was interesting. The village is about four miles out the back gate. Seven U.S. men live there in a small ARVN compound with maybe 60 Arvins. For three days they were surrounded by a battalion of VC—with the help of chopper gunships they were able to hold out—but air strikes did destroy about 200 huts and houses. So there are lots of refugees there. Luckily few civilians were killed in this village, as opposed to Saigon, where according to our reports there must be tremendous suffering among the civilians. Of the 75–100 people who came to Med Cap today I saw no injuries from the fighting. But I did walk through the village and see people trying to save old roof tiles and sheets of tin—and family possessions. One little mentally and physically retarded boy of eight or 10 took my hand and walked down the dirt road with me. Here would be a straw hut with water buffalo in the front yard, then a pile of ashes and tin, then two or three more such piles. At one of them the little boy stopped, pointed at the pile and then himself. It had been his family home, they lost everything but themselves.

Well it's now too dark to see any longer so I'll quit—

My love to all,
Bill

BARBARA J. LILLY *served in Vietnam from March 1968 to March 1969 as a civilian with the American Red Cross Supplemental Recreational Activities Overseas program, also known as the "Donut Dollies," in Phan Rang, Lai Khe, Cam Ranh, II Field Forces, and other temporary assignments. Upon her return to the United States, she volunteered with the Vietnam Women's Memorial Project for 13 years. Barbara sent the following letters to her parents, Leonard and Mary Dorr, who were living in Detroit, Michigan.*

Thursday, March 1968
Saigon

Today we got ID cards and ration cards for the PX. We got two noncombatant ID cards and supposedly if you're captured by the Cong you give them one and keep one. That's about the biggest laugh I've ever heard. "One for me, one for you."

April 20th
Lai Khe

Today I had a great experience. A company just came in from the field and they asked if we'd go serve them ice cream. We got there too late to greet the choppers but pulled up in a jeep as they were sitting around on the ground finishing chow. They were still all dirty and everything but grinned like crazy when they saw us. It was so great for us because the officer said they really needed a morale boost (the men did). There were 80 in the company when they went out three days ago and 37 of them are left. Actually they didn't grin at first—they were shocked. Then they warmed up with the ice cream as an ice breaker, and then after we'd talked to them awhile they began to act embarrassed because of their appearance. A couple times I thought I'd cry but under the circumstances the easiest and yet the hardest thing to do is smile. Some of the guys had tears in their eyes and you just want to hold their hand or something so you just smile. The saddest part of it all was they were shot by our own gunships! Only four dead and seven wounded were VC doing. They don't know what gunships they were. But they weren't the Robin Hoods. They have the best reputation for no mistakes.

Yesterday afternoon we took ice cream to the hospitals. That was really rewarding, too. While we were at the one they brought in a wounded guy by dust-off. That's the first time I'd seen one before they're cleaned up. I was surprised it didn't make me sick or anything—just made you feel helpless.

CAPTAIN EDWARD ALLEN BOARDMAN *was a veteran of World War Two and Korea when he departed for Vietnam in August 1967. He wrote to his wife and six children every other day while serving in Vietnam. He was awarded the Vietnamese Order of Gallantry, the Army Commendation Medal, the Bronze Star, and the Purple Heart.*

*Captain Boardman died early in the morning of April 1, 1968, of burns received during a mortar attack. All of his hootchmates died with him except the chaplain, who was on R&R in Japan. Captain Boardman is buried in Arlington National Cemetery.*

Thursday Eve.

7 Mar 68

8:15 P.M.

My Beloved Family,

Some nights (and days) a guy just gets homesick—even an old soldier like me—and tonight is one of those times. If I close my eyes I can just hear all the "sounds of home," kitchen, TV, kids fights between Carol and Jamie, etc. Sure would give the world to be there. But, on the bright side, I did get a letter from you today, June. It's been about four days and I was quite worried inasmuch as in your last letter you had mentioned having the "bug" and in your previous letter you told about your back bothering you again. I received your Letter of 2 March, one with Lent Program. Earlier this week I got a letter from your mom and also from a young man stationed with an Engr. Unit over here who your mom had given my address. Anyway, I replied and invited him to stop in if he had the chance. His unit used to be in Bearcat (9th Div Base Camp) but I think his unit has moved into the Delta as most of the 9th is in that area at that moment.

Since Monday night (when we got the 10 rockets) it has been fairly quiet. It is never truly quiet, but speaking relatively, it's been fairly so.

Thursday Eve
/ 7 Mar 68
8:15 PM

My Beloved Family,

Some nights (and days) a guy just gets homesick — even an old soldier like me and tonight is one of those times — if I close my eyes I can just hear all the "sounds of home" — kitchen — TV, kids fights between Carlo Jamie, etc. Sure would give the world to be there. But, on the brighter side, I did get a letter today from you June — it's been about 4 days and I was quite worried inasmuch as in your last letter you had mentioned having the "bug" and in your previous letter you told about your back bothering you again — I received your letter of 2 March — one with Lent program. Earlier this week I got a letter from your Mom and also from a young man stationed with Eng Unit over here who your Mom had given my address. Anyway — I replied and invited him to stop in if he had the chance — his unit used to be below me in Bearcat (9th Div Base Camp) but I think his unit has moved into the Delta as most of 9th is in that area at the moment.

Since Monday Nite (when we got the 10 rocket) it has been "fairly" quiet — it is never truly quiet

Sent Andrea a card this P.M., almost forgot, it's hell to have to look at a calendar to see what DAY it is, let alone the date. Anyway I was signing some military requisitions when I noticed the date. Then bought a card and got it in the mail.

George is good, as are all of Hut 4. George and I had hoped to go to Hawaii at the same time, however, his mother-in-law won't arrive to care for their children until about 20 June so they are planning on/about 25 June for their R&R.

All my problems last night were ones involving individual soldiers. Had two men last night go completely berserk. One a Mexican guy who I've given every break there was. Had a bad record prior to here, been in stockade, anyway I accepted him as a rehabilitative transfer and he almost made it. He *was* due to rotate 6 April. He got drunk, disrespectful to Lt. Drews, disorderly and drunk in camp and a whole host of others. Writing charges on him this P.M. when I sent Andrea's card. His father served 14 years on a life term when he died so you can see his background. Anyway, two hrs with Trijillio last night getting him in line and then about 1:00 A.M. they brought another colored kid up for me out of the depot. Anyway he was scared, screaming prejudice, and anything else that came to mind. Put him in psychiatric ward for evaluation. He came to me TDY for security guard and I don't have Court Martial jurisdiction over him but will provide his CO with statements, etc. to do with as he pleases. Of course, had to get a replacement from the CO of his unit and I'm sure the one they sent isn't of much different caliber. Not many volunteers for this ammo dump, everybody afraid of it and I can't say that I much blame them.

Well my dearest ones, will try and get some sleep early again tonight as last nite all went to pot. I'm feeling pretty good although stomach still bothers at night, tension and all don't contribute to a quiet stomach.

Nite my dear children, beloved wife

Always & all ways,

XXXXX

OOOO

Your guy,

Ed

Sure hope your check wasn't too late although I know mail wasn't going out as they implied it was.

*Captain Edward Allen Boardman*
*(photo by his hoochmate, Captain Blaylock,*
*with Edward's Polaroid camera)*

Specialist 5th Class Bill McCloud *wrote the following letter to his parents, describing one of the "characters" he knew. His letter also includes an answer to an earlier question from his mother about how many people they carried in their helicopters, and tells the travails of his buddy, Tim.*

30 Sep 68
Mon. Mor.
Day 189

Dear Mom & Dad—

September is almost "all gone."

We've got a guy in our hootch that is something else. His name is Ralph. He is fun to be with and funny to listen to. Since he has been in Vietnam, about 10 months, he has been busted from Specialist Fourth Class to Private, been fined $150 and had 28 days extra duty. He isn't a bad guy, he just doesn't like the Army. He gets drunk all the time, but is not a hostile drunk. One time he was too drunk to go on guard duty and they fined him and gave him extra duty. The other time he had taken a truck from the motor pool and two cases of fruit and had been caught going into the South Vietnamese Army's women's compound with all kinds of wild ideas. He's crazy!

The 54th Aviation Company is right next to us and they had a pet duck. He wandered over into our area yesterday and Ralph and another guy caught it, chopped off its head, plucked it, and it is now in our mess hall's refrigerator. Ralph says he loves to eat duck!

We carry 33 Americans and their gear in one load. That's how many seats we have. If we carry South Vietnamese soldiers we get about 55 in, and one time we carried little Vietnamese children and got about 94 of them in. They had the time of their life.

Poor Tim, my roommate, sure has problems. He has about a month and a half left. A couple of months ago he put in his request for duty when he leaves Vietnam. He requested Fort Rucker, Alabama, because his girlfriend lives less than 100 miles from there. I've seen pictures of her and she is beautiful. Well, out of about 20 guys that put in their requests at the same time, he is the only one of them that got the station they asked for. Now get this! Two days after he put in his request he got a letter from her and found out her father had been transferred to California. They are now settled in California and Tim can't believe his good-bad luck. Then he got a letter from her today and she wants to join the Navy so she can be close to him. You have to admire the reason, but the idea is ridiculous. She doesn't realize what she will be getting into. He is writing her now to tell her not to, definitely not to! He just hopes on the spur of the moment she doesn't go and join. If he could talk to her in person there wouldn't be any problem, but . . .

Love to all,

Billy

*He wrote the following letter home to his mother at the beginning of 1969.*

Happy New Year, Mom—

I sure enjoyed the Bob Hope show. I went to Dong Tam to see it because he didn't bring the show here. I was unbelievably lucky. I got to sit in the third row of seats right next to the center side. There were about five rows of guys sitting in front of me. I couldn't believe it when I actually got the seat up there. The radio said there were 30,000 soldiers at the show.

I got to see Bob Hope, Ann-Margret, Miss World, and about 17 other girls.

I left here a nobody and came back a living legend. I got to talk to Ann-Margret. I saw the show on the 27th and they still haven't stopped asking about her.

I happened to catch her a half hour after the show when there was no one with her but a colonel, so I got to have a nice quick talk with her for a little over five minutes.

I got to shake her hand and she autographed a picture for me and all that good stuff.

She asked me to forgive her for perspiring and said a woman should always glow. She said she hoped she can see me when I come home, and every morning I wake up and tell myself that she was serious. Boy, am I a dreamer.

She has a very soft hand and very pretty hair. I realized I've been over here quite awhile, but I think she is the sexiest person I have ever seen. She was fantastic on stage and great in person.

One of our pilots was jumped downtown last week by two Vietnamese civilians. They asked him for his billfold and he politely refused, so they proceeded to pounce on him. One had a club and the other had a knife. He held his own for a few minutes, then managed to break away from them and get an MP. They took him to the hospital and X-rayed for skull fracture, but everything was alright. He has about three knife cuts on his face, but they aren't deep.

I followed Apollo 8 closely. It was quite an adventure.

Is Betty's hair growing long now or not?

I'll write again soon and be home almost as soon.

Love,<br>Billy

COLONEL ROBERT E. TSCHAN *wrote the following letter to his* *then–penpal, now wife, Kathryn H. Deising.*

24 April '68

Dear Dee,

Please excuse the long delay in my answers. I feel guilty getting so many letters, packages, etc., and not being able to write more often. Your letters and the Easter candy and book are really appreciated.

I received your packages and a letter yesterday and a card and letter today. Your latest card is very timely and really outstanding. I got a real kick out of it. As for it being timely—well, I guess that's up to "Charlie." I have five more days before I depart Hue, one night in Da Nang, and three days and nights in Saigon before I jump on the flight to civilization. The doom reports have been coming in in large quantity and pretty reliable quality that the final phase of the VC/NVA offensive is to begin some time between tonight and the 28th. This unfortunately will include a massive ground attack on Hue and similar on Ton Son Nhut Air Base— from which my flight to San Francisco departs.

I hate to sound pessimistic but—damn—why me with only five more days? Everyone gets jumpy just prior to leaving country, guess I'm no different. If the news hasn't reported any significant happenings by the time you get this letter, I'll probably be very near to boarding my plane at 0715 on 03 May. Anything after that, count me out! At least until approx. 20 June or so.

I shall attempt to keep you informed of my trip via postcard. What can I say?

You mentioned the delicacies of Thailand—ha—you'd never believe the Vietnamese delicacies. I'll give you a try with an explanation of some of the normal every day dishes. Keep in mind that I've had amoebic dysentery twice, worms, and Dengue Fever since my arrival. First off, chicken—it's prepared by first getting about 90%

of the feathers off, then the entire chicken, and I mean ENTIRE, is chopped up like diced ham, cooked and served—head, eyes, stomach, legs (feet also), bones, etc., are eaten. The blood is scraped off to one side and we have coagulated chicken blood pudding or duck pudding, boiled duck embryo, peanuts, and a putrid rice paste. Along with this goes swamp water tea or beer or rice wine, depending on the occasion. Anything you can't chew or get down, you spit out on the dirt floor. The Vietnamese spit out very little, but the advisors end up either giving in to their "manners" or to custom and spit out nearly everything or else getting most of a "polite" amount down and await an opportunity to slip away and get it all up at once. Hope you don't get this letter before dinner!

The first time I tried Vietnamese food I forced myself. After five days I got dysentery and during the next ten days I lost 30 lbs. Enough of the hardships.

Great!!! I'll probably draw combat pay and get medals and all that crap on my next tour of duty—STATESIDE! Chicago, Detroit, Baltimore, Washington, D.C. etc., sound bad. I definitely agree with the Mayor of Chicago—if they jump out of line, zap!! I am very much ashamed of some of the actions that have occurred in the U.S. recently. I guess I'm a "hawk" at home and abroad.

I've got to work tomorrow, and seeing that I have the duty tonight and can't get any sleep I'm not looking forward to facing my tasks in the morning.

I'll close for now and try to get off another letter to you just before I leave Saigon. My next correspondence will be mailed from Oslo—I hope.

Bob

P.S. Haven't started your book yet, however, if I have a quiet night on duty, I'll attempt—with an open mind!

LIEUTENANT PAT BRANTLEY, *a nurse with the 36th Evacuation Hospital in Vietnam, describes some of the voluntary medical work she and other members of her hospital did with the Vietnamese villagers.*

July 18, 1966

Dear Folks,

This is my third day off in a row! Today was my Fourth of July holiday. I spent the afternoon on the beach.

Yesterday was one of the most rewarding days I've ever spent since I've been here. I went on a junk (a Vietnamese boat) to a small fishing village south of here on the coast with Med Cap (Medical Civil Action Program). It's strictly voluntary on off-duty time, and they go up every Sunday. It's set up by the Navy. Five nurses, two doctors, and the dentist with our hospital went yesterday. We take medicines and supplies along, and set up a clinic right outdoors for anybody who needs to come—and, believe me, they come! I've never washed so many babies and children in my life! They had so many sores, a lot from just lack of using soap and water. Then we applied Furacin ointment. A lot of people had infected places and we gave out antibiotic pills, etc. We had an interpreter along to tell them how to take them and to tell the doctors the symptoms. Several of the other girls had been on previous Sundays, and I had been wanting to go. It was just wonderful!

The village itself had no paved streets, all sand, and there were huge black fishing nets strung up all over to dry. . . .

Major Robert B. MacKenzie's *Vietnam tour lasted from July 1968 to August 1969. He was the Assistant Chief of Staff, G2 of Task Force Hotel, with headquarters at Fire Support Base Vanderbrift in the mountains just below the DMZ in I Corps. His honors include the Vietnamese Cross of Gallantry with Gold Star.*

*He wrote the following letters, which describe Marine and Army operations in I Corps, to his wife, Linnea B. MacKenzie.*

25 June, 1968

Return address:

G2 Section, 3dMarDiv, FPO San Fran 96628

Ignore my address on this morning's letter. It appears as though I'm not going there. Mike Spark wants me to work for him. I've just left his office and will be going back to see him this evening.

I'm writing this at Wayne's desk. He thought you'd like to know he's taking care of me properly.

Rode up on the plane from Da Nang with John Rokis. He's working for Wayne and is about 10 feet from me as I write this.

Saw Dick Stacey this morning at chow, and have come across another classmate from Quantico. Two sergeants from Force Recon work up in the G2. Two of my boys from Bremerhaven are here with Meech. I could leave this place now and be perfectly happy, for I think I've seen everyone I've ever known in the past two days. I just missed Lt. Col. Blyth on the phone in Da Nang, but I'm sure I'll see him later.

Here at Dong Ha it's a shambles from fairly constant mortar attacks. The holes are quickly mended, though, and life goes on as usual. This is a barren, dusty, *hot,* windy place that no one but an armed force would ever want. I can look out the front door of the bunker and see the firing off in the hills two miles or so away. And it is *HOT!*

Will write when I find out where I'll be.

Still have no final determination as to my ultimate disposition, but am trying to stay as much ahead of Michael Spark as I can. He likes me and all that jazz, but if I goof up I'll just be another man to add to the relief rolls.

Have been wandering around up here in Dong Ha and in Quang Tri asking questions of everyone who might seem to have answers to what's troubling my curious little mind, and in the process, of course, I've seen still more friends. Sam came up from Da Nang yesterday and is living right across the street here in the 3d Division Headquarters area. He'll take over the 15th CIT shortly. It seems to be a fine team, for I've had several long hours of conversation over there on one thing or another. Ed Turner (from El Toro) is there, so I had a chance to catch up on many of the people who have been through here.

I must have been some sort of good omen for this place, for there have been no rockets or shells land in this area since I got here. We see the firing a few miles outside the perimeter, of course, but it doesn't really affect us here in the relative security of the command post. It does seem strange to me to realize that only a week ago I was saying goodbye to you in Monterey.

I finally got a full night's sleep last night, after averaging perhaps five hours a night for the past week—perhaps the heat, the strange circumstances, the rather tense position I'm in—all might have something to do with it. The rats around our tent don't help too much, either.

They've rigged a shower up using the belly tank from one of the fighter-bombers, so I've been able to keep relatively clean—at least at night after the dust and wind stop blowing. I'm gradually becoming acclimated, too, so the tremendous heat isn't affecting me quite as severely as last week. Still, I understand the worst is to come, so I'm girding myself mentally for 120 degree heat.

I'm looking forward greatly to your first letter, so I'll be particularly happy to get settled in one place or the other as soon as possible. I can already feel the kids growing up in my absence and can visualize the type of trouble you may be having with them.

Have decided that Hawaii is the place for the R&R, so you'll have to get suitable clothing for me and bring it with you when you come. All I'll have is the tropical uniform I step off the aircraft in. Am already looking forward to it immensely, even though I know it won't be for several more months yet.

13 July

Was supposed to have gone on an operation this morning (my first) with the PRUs—a bunch of convicts, murderers, rapists: in short, *real* hoods. For all their destructive proclivities, they are reputed to be the finest troops in Viet Nam now, for they are true mercenaries—they fight only for money and the love of fighting. If I had to equate them to anything, I'd have to say that they're about on a par, though possibly of better quality, with the Amphib Recon Co. of MMS back in '56.

Well, anyway, the operation could not be mounted because of a lack of coordination with American Army units, so it is definitely on for tomorrow. I shall be on my way as I mail this letter.

The PRUs are recruited from the civil and military prisons, and I am very much looking forward to seeing them perform. They are the government's "elimination" force, and their primary job is the assassination of VC. Tomorrow we'll be going into an area in the south part of the hamlet to capture (for a change—usually they're kill on the spot) two VC who are supposed to be hiding in the village. Despite constant harassment by our forces, the VC still have controlled this village for five years, so no one really knows what to expect.

Accordingly, despite what the general rules of warfare say, tomorrow I'll be armed with a 12-gauge shotgun and six grenades. My jeep will have a machine gun mounted in it, and we'll all still carry our submachine guns and pistols besides.

I'm not trying to scare you a bit—just trying to let you know how things can change rapidly in a short time. Last week I was sitting in the MACV compound fat, dumb, and happy. Now I'm with the PRU for a bit. MMS has me jumping quite a bit.

The "Doom Reports" for Quang Tri continue to come in, though the Army here seems to take little action to prevent what most certainly, if it comes off, will be *the* major battle in this province since Tet. I'll tell you—I'm not particularly looking forward to relying on the Army for protection. Really, with all this warning of impending catastrophe, no one has really done a damn thing to improve defenses or take preventive measure to keep the VC and NVA out of here. I'm nervous, Kiddo.

Well, enough gloom for tonight. As I look back briefly on what I've written, I see that I've perhaps understated our state of preparedness. We do have rather substantial bunkers to fight from, and we are surrounded by barbed wire and mine fields. If they try to get in here, they'll leave at least 200 bodies in the wire. They may not be willing to take that kind of casualties for what after all would only be a moral victory. Strategically, Quang Tri's only importance is that it sits alongside the only north-south highway in the country. And we can mount absolutely devastating air and artillery attacks. They couldn't possibly hold the city for more than a few hours. When they attacked here during Tet, they lost about 1,500 men. They'll lose at least that many if they try it next week.

SERGEANT HOWARD QUERRY *of Downers Grove, Illinois, was drafted in August 1966 into the U.S. Army. According to his wife, Pauline Laurent, Sergeant Querry immediately went to see an Army recruiter who promised him that if he enlisted for an extra year, he would guarantee him an administrative job. He enlisted in the Army and after basic and advanced infantry training was accepted into Officer Candidate School. After 18 weeks of OCS, he was kicked out because he was told he wasn't forceful enough to become an infantry officer. He was then sent to NCOC, which was a training school for sergeants headed for Vietnam. On March 11, 1968, he shipped out to Vietnam. He was stationed in the Mekong Delta at Fort Courage, an old French fort, with the 9th Infantry Division. He wrote 21 letters to his wife, the last one postmarked May 3, 1968.*

*Sergeant Querry was killed on May 10, 1968, in the Gia Dinh province as he was leading his squad across a bridge. His wife, seven months pregnant at the time, was notified on May 15, five days after his death, and his remains were brought to the states on May 23 with the coffin marked "Non-Viewable."*

*His numerous honors include the Good Conduct Medal, the National Defense Service Medal, and the Purple Heart. His wife, Pauline, is the author of* Grief Denied: A Vietnam Widow's Story *(www.griefdenied.com).*

*He wrote the following letters to his wife.*

*Sergeant Howard Querry (killed in Vietnam;*
*photographer unknown)*

April 3, 1968

Hi Honey,

What have you been doing that is interesting and exciting? I haven't been doing anything interesting but I'm getting plenty of excitement.

I made a tape for you last night so I don't really have any other news. I just thought I'd let you know that I'm thinking about you everyday and every night. In fact I think about you all the time. I sure do miss you and I sure wish I had some pictures of you. You said you were going to send me some but you haven't yet.

This place sure is sickening. You are always dirty. If it's not dusty, it's muddy, so you can never keep clean. And, the people over here are really sickening. They urinate in the streets and poop in the streets. They breastfeed their babies in the streets. They just turn my stomach. The kids run up to you and ask for candy and gum and while they are asking you, they try to steal your watch, your pens, your wallet, and everything you've got. I almost broke one kid's arm when he tried to steal my watch. It's really disgusting around here at times.

Everybody thinks that Saigon is so neat. I thought it was kind of dumpy. There is trash all over the streets and dirt roads. I can't wait until I get back home to you and the baby and Arfie.

I have to run down to the gook laundry pretty soon so they can wash some of the scum off my clothes.

I think I'm going to take a pro pay test while I'm over here so I can make about $30 or $40 a month more.

That wonderful Johnson stopped the bombing again I heard. He is really an idiot! I also heard he wasn't running for President, so now I guess they'll run that wonderful Kennedy. I'm still going to vote for Nixon. How about you? I do think Nixon is the best man. Enough about that. You already know what I think about it so I better not say anything else or I'll just get all excited again.

Oh, I forgot to tell you about my moustache. All the NCOs and officers in the company have one so they informed me that I should start growing mine. I've been working on it for about four days and it's really a scream. I don't know if I'm going to like the idea or not because it might start itching and if it does, it is coming off immediately if not sooner.

I'm beginning to look like a Beatle now too because I haven't had a haircut since I left Ft. Jackson. Barbers are rare birds around here. I sure am getting black from the sun over here.

Have you been changing the oil in the car and the spark plugs and all that stuff? I don't remember whether we got new spark plugs before we made our trip. Did we?

I sure wish I could feel the baby kicking around inside you. Does it kick all the time? Maybe it is nervous like me, you think? They say if it's a boy, they kick a lot, don't they? What should we name the other one if it's twins?

Well Honey, I better clean up my equipment 'cause we are going out again today in a few hours. It's just a small operation this time though.

Take care of yourself, the baby & Arfie. You have all my love and kisses—I'm saving them all up for Hawaii. I love you so much, Darling.

All my love,
Howard

Easter Sunday
April 14, 1968

Hi Honey,

I'm real happy today because I got four letters from you. I was so happy to hear that you are working at Scott AFB. Does your job make time pass a little faster? I hope it does 'cause I know how you feel.

Sometimes, I get so lonesome for you that I could cry. When we are out on an operation it is much easier 'cause then I'm too worried about coming back that night and I'm not lonesome. Everybody out there is thinking the same thing that I am. I carry my wallet with me and look at your picture wherever I go.

Yes, I heard Johnson's speech but I won't believe it until the election. I think it might be another one of his tricks to get more votes. Anyway, whether he runs or not, I'm still going to vote for Nixon because I can't stand Rockefeller and Nixon knows what is going on. Another thing that impresses me is that he is running again after being beaten before. By the same token, I don't think he'll quit until he does something about this war and the world situation. I haven't run into anyone over here who would have voted for Johnson. You're right, I didn't like the bombing pause—especially since it has been almost two weeks and they can't decide where they are going to have their peace talks.

This war just turns my stomach. It seems like a big political game and I feel that American lives are not to be played with. Another thing, I feel that if they do have their peace talks and succeed, it will be just like Korea and in another 10 years we will be back here fighting again. I say bomb the hell out of North Viet Nam & we won't have to worry 'bout 10 years from now.

They are still debating on moving us out of the Fort permanently. I don't really think they will. At least I hope not.

I have to go to sleep now because I'm just so tired because we stumbled through mud up to our knees all day today. I'm on radio watch now and my time is just about up. Have a Happy Easter, Honey. I'll be thinking about you all day.

Please take care of yourself and the baby and don't eat too much today. O.K.? I love you Darling with all my heart and soul. You have

All my love,

Howard

*An envelope containing a letter written by Pauline Laurent to her husband, Sgt. Howard Querry, in Vietnam. Note "Verified DECEASED, RETURN TO SENDER" indication.*

COMMANDER EUGENE JOSEPH RICE *served in the U.S. Navy during World War Two, completed flight training, and flew in Europe during the war and in Africa just after the war. His honors include the National Defense Service Medal and the Navy Occupation Service Medal. Commander Rice died in May 2000 and, according to his wishes, his ashes were scattered over the ocean from a U.S. Navy plane. Commander Rice was retired from the Navy and a civilian with Informatics, assigned to Headquarters MACV (DMA) and living in Vietnam from August to December 1968 when he wrote the following letters to his 21-year-old daughter, Colonel Mary Jo Rice. She was beginning her career as a U.S. Army nurse and in five months would report for duty in Vietnam.*

Sunday 1 Sept. 1968

My Dearest Mary Jo,

Greetings from Saigon. We have been here a month, and, although the days seem to drag, working six or seven days a week and living more or less as a group has helped to speed the days by. We have a fine group of people and we spend quite a large part of the days and evenings together to help stave off the "Missing the Folks Feeling."

I spent a wonderful day with Col. Sol Codispoti and just returned from a two-day visit to the Attack Carrier USS *America.* We attended the preflight briefing of the young Navy pilots before they manned their planes for night strikes against the North Vietnamese. We then went up to the signal bridge, six levels above the flight deck, and watched those brave young men take off in the black night—it was like a scene from Dante's Inferno. The screaming, thunderous roar of the jets packed on the flight deck is so intense that one has to wear thick insulated plastic ear muffs to avoid permanent ear damage. Even at six levels above the flight deck, the searing, hot noxious exhaust of the jets turning up with full afterburner on the catapults would force us to duck behind a steel shield and hold our breath. My prayers went with every lad who took off, and that mighty ship of 80,000 tons shuddered as the catapults let go.

We had a lot of work to do and we were up until five A.M. in the morning. We were up at eight to have breakfast and catch our plane back to Saigon. During the night we went topside again to watch the night recovery of the returning strike. These high performance jets hit the deck at about 150 miles per hour. They have only four steel arresting cables to catch with their tail hooks, and it is an operation fraught with danger. They come down with full power under the control of the landing signal officer (LSO) back on the fan tail. He has the full authority to wave them off for another try or O.K. the landing. Many times they hit the deck and fail to catch a wire and around they go again into the black night hoping to God they put it down the next time. After the recovery we went down to the pilots debriefing room and watched these exhausted young men come in drenched with sweat from head to toe. They told the intelligence types what targets they dropped on and described the quantity and types of antiaircraft fire they experienced. It was an awesome, breathtaking experience which I will never forget. Those young men are truly among the bravest in the land, as are those out fighting day and night in the rice paddies and the tropical jungle.

Saigon is a war swollen city with refugees living in the streets. The dirt, filth, and odors with which these people have to live, in abject poverty, makes one realize how remarkably blessed is the USA and how fortunate we are to be living there.

We have a curfew from 10 P.M. to 6 A.M. and it is deemed very advisable to allow plenty of time to get home before the curfew. There are soldiers behind barbed wire emplacements at every corner, and due to the many constant terrorist incidents they are a bit trigger happy. People are shot down in the streets, grenades are thrown into jeeps, bombs are placed in public buildings, and rockets are indiscriminately fired into the city in a mad attempt to break the will and morale of the civilian populace. The doves back home,

McCarthy, Fulbright, and the rest of them, should get their asses out here and see the nature and brutality of the enemy we are fighting.

A short while ago I had occasion to visit the 3rd Army Field Hospital just outside of the air base, Ton San Nhut. I walked into what was the outpatient clinic and there through a wide open portal I saw them operating on a young soldier with a serious chest wound—no curtain to block off the operating room. The lad had just been flown in by helicopter from the battlefield. I hoped and prayed that he made it.

I guess that by this time you have heard from the State Board and that you have your orders to San Antone (spelling?). You are starting out on a magnificent voyage through life and you are well equipped for it with intelligence, character, a precious sense of humor, and training.

Good luck—do good—I have a tear in my eye as I'm writing to you.

Love,

Dad

*Colonel Rice received the following letter from her father while she was a second lieutenant in Army nurse basic training at Fort Sam Houston, Texas.*

9/26/68

My Dearest Lieutenant,

The top of this immortal day to you and "How the Hell are you?" Your letters are a source of deep enjoyment and I truly feel that I am a man "most blessed" with the children I have. Your letters literally sing of "life" and it is fitting and right. Every young person's heart should sing.

By this time you have probably gotten over the feeling of being a recruit and may perhaps have progressed to the advanced stage of barracks bitching? It's all wonderful and lots of the gripes are right.

I was magnificent at it. I remember telling the troops in the Navy barracks at Floyd Bennett Field that I was going to fly my flight instructor into the side of the hangar just to kill the monster (a magnificent Marine). One time on a takeoff I was banking the plane rather steeply and he said, "Did I teach you to climb out of a field and warp up the plane in a steep bank?" Being a lowly recruit I answered, "No sir," and he replied, "O.K., Lindbergh, straighten it out!"

Never fear what you don't know. Be eager to learn—but never volunteer. We had an expression in the Navy, "Keep your bowels open, your mouth shut, and never volunteer."

In my travels over here, Mary Jo, I have visited three Navy Task Force operations "in-country" in Vietnam. In the Mobile Riverine Force, which is an outfit composed of river gunboats and troop carrying craft, I found a bunch of young heroes. Their casualty rate is beyond belief. They take their gunboat flotilla up narrow rivers where the VC are waiting for them in prepared ambushes. Within moments they are under withering fire, fight their way to a landing spot, unload the Army troops who go ashore taking severe losses and never quit until they have routed the enemy. They may fight for five or six days in the rice paddies in six inches of water before they better the enemy, and they never quit. They suffer terribly from immersion foot during these engagements and their feet become so swollen and blistered so as to render them casualties. It was truly inspiring to see these young soldiers and sailors. I wished I could be with them. For every callow, young man back in the states who feels no love of country there are a thousand out here who, not knowing all the reasons why, are ready to see the job through and have an intuitive faith in what is right or what is wrong. Our Senators and other leaders back home could well take a lesson.

Well, my Dearest Mary Jo, I've finished my sea stories. I miss you so, and I long for the sight and sound of you. Be of good cheer

and strong faith. Be sure of yourself—warm, loving, and under-
standing toward others, and in addition be a fine Irishman.

I love you,

Dad

P.S. Dear M.J. is it necessary to put that big long number after your
name?

BRENDA RODGERS *wrote the following letter home to her parents,*
*Dr. and Mrs. Rosen, who were living in University City, a suburb of*
*St. Louis, in Missouri. Ms. Rodgers married Major Hal Rodgers,*
*whom she had met in Saigon but whose hometown of Madisonville,*
*Kentucky, is only 250 miles away from St. Louis. The letter describes*
*their marriage in Saigon on April 23, 1970. While her parents had*
*been wondering about their intentions for over a year, Brenda and*
*Hal had been battling U.S. red tape having to do with living quarters*
*and her job with the U.S. Agency for International Development,*
*which did not allow a spouse in-country. They were perhaps the first*
*couple from USAID and the Army to marry.*

*Brenda and Major Hal Rodgers on their wedding day,*
*Saigon City Hall, April 23, 1970 (photo taken by*
*unknown photographer with Brenda's camera)*

May 2, 1970 A.M. (after marriage)

Hi,

Well, this is the old married lady of one week reporting in. I've been meaning all week to write the particulars of the wedding day, but until now I've had no chance. I guess if the social column of the *Post* were to cover it, it would read something like this.

The marriage ceremony of Major Harold L. Rodgers and Miss Brenda R. Rosen took place on the second floor ball room of Saigon City Hall on April 23, 1970. The bride wore the tattered green and yellow dress of two years ago and carried three cameras with flash attachments. The groom matched the bride by also wearing the same clothes that he had on the day they met. Those fatigues were beautifully starched and the polish on his combat boots couldn't help but be reflected in the radiant sunshine of the day.

The ceremony lasted all of five minutes and was performed in both English and Vietnamese. Presiding over the occasion was the District Chief of Saigon's First Precinct. More than 75 chairs were lined up, but the stubborn bride had only a handful of individuals in attendance. That had occurred after the Mayor of Saigon felt guilty about not allowing the wedding in his study because weddings were bad luck in Vietnamese culture to the extent that it would spoil his day's work. Funerals were good luck but they did not want that. So he surprised them with the ballroom and told all health employees to attend. The bride then shared American tradition with the Mayor, explaining brides get their way on their day. The city employees were then informed to stay at work, and the bride had her small circle of wanted and necessary attendees.

Among the witnesses were Dr. Canh and Miss Collins. Dr. Canh has been counterpart to Miss Rosen and close friend to both the bride and groom for two years. Miss Collins is the individual responsible for introducing the couple to each other. Also on hand was the Chief Health Officer for the city, the Secretary General of the city, and the sour faded old maid representative who was necessary from the U.S. Consulate.

The ceremony was concluded when the couple kissed at the wrong time, the bride put her rings on backwards, and the groom couldn't even get the ring on his finger.

Following the wedding, Dr. Canh took the couple and Miss Collins out for late morning coffee after getting rid of the U.S. representative in a taxi. The coffee clutch was highlighted when the Army groom produced a flask of scotch out of his hip pocket, an Air Force flask no less.

The new couple then went off by themselves to place an overseas call to St. Louis. While waiting and praying the call would go through from the land of you never know, the bride and groom took off for a bowl of pho (local soup) at one of the sidewalk potential ptomaine palaces.

The phone call went through fairly well and sighs of relief were heard on both sides of the world. In Vietnam the sighs were of relief because the collect charges were accepted. In St. Louis the noise was also of relief for after a year the bride's family was beginning to wonder about this relationship that had included some overnights without a wedding band. The brother in St. Louis was so ecstatic that he told his patients that his sister got married tomorrow. His patients told him his English stunk, but he told them his English was fine and their geography stunk. Oh, the dateline, how it does confuse.

Then the couple headed for the bride's old residence, where they will reside *when* the Colonel lets the groom come into Saigon *if* USAID does not throw them out.

They had hoped to consummate the marriage immediately. However, a pending party which had been thought up over the scotch, and the day maid's presence, somehow prevented passion. The remainder of the afternoon was spent in preparation for the impromptu gathering.

The party began at 1630 when the ice showed up in the capable hands of two Captains. It continued until midnight when the couple had to take the last two intoxicated guests home after curfew. Over 50 people showed up, and although "no gifts" was specified on the phone invites, individuals still showed up bearing such lovely items as intrauterine devices.

After freezing the remains of the cake, the couple "passed out" quietly.

The following morning at 0600 the couple left for a three day honeymoon at the oceanside city of Nha Trang. What happened there, we are not sure. We do know they were traveling under false orders, to an unauthorized area, and using different names.

Yep Folks, that's about the story. Oh, I failed to mention how beautiful the cake was. Hal had it made out at Summer Camp. It was white and pink with three layers plus an additional layer of soot and dust from being brought in on the highway in an open jeep.

Love you,
The Major and the Mrs. (Thieu Ta and Ba Thieu Ta)

*In this letter, CS1. James C. Kline, U.S. Navy, of Anaheim, California, tries to explain to his only child, Ricky, age seven, the burdens and responsibilities of a soldier and a father.*

March 14, 1966
Camp Tien-Sha
Da Nang, Vietnam

A letter to my son,

Ricky, my son, this will not be an easy letter for me to write because I may use some of the wrong words or I may not be able to make you understand the meaning of this letter.

You are still a young man yet and the world looks awfully big and mysterious to you, and a lot of things happen to you that you don't understand, but someday you will have a son of your own and you will have these feelings as I have tonight. At least I hope you do.

You probably can't understand why I must be away from you, over here, missing all the good times we've had together and seeing you grow up as the days go by, but I feel that my duty and responsibility to you starts with making the world a little safer, I hope and pray, for you and your son (you may have someday) to grow up in. You also have a responsibility, and that is for you to take advantage of these opportunities that are made available to you. These are some of the rules that I have used to help me, and you might want to use them, too. First of all: Believe in God and follow his commandments; be loyal, trustworthy, morally clean, and spiritually right. Never lie no matter what, honor and love and respect your mother and father. Respect the rights and property of others. Do not covet what belongs to others, do not steal, and do not use the word and the name of God in vain.

Jesus had a cross to bear and all of us over here have our cross to bear. We may falter but must carry the load ourselves as Jesus did, but we can call on him any time the load gets too heavy or we need help. There are a lot of fathers here that are making their sacrifice so that their sons and you may have a free country to grow up in—to have the right to worship as you choose and to make of yourself as you see fit. These are only simple things to you and me. But there are very few people in this world who have this right. Cherish it! You have a good home, wonderful mother and many good friends, and above all else, you have God.

I miss you and your mother so very, very much and I look forward anxiously to the day when we can all be together again and enjoy one another. Be a good boy and I want you to know that I'm the proudest and the luckiest father in the world to have such a fine son as you. I'm glad you chose me to be your father.

Give your mother a big hug and kiss for me and remember you are the man of the house while I'm away. I know you are helping your mother and making things easier for her. You must do this because she has an awful lot on her mind and a lot of work to do to see that things run smooth. Remember me and all the others over here in your prayers at night and ask Him to help people see the folly of all this fighting and bickering that goes on in this troubled world. Above all I want you to know that I'm proud that I have a chance to do my part to make all of these things available to you. Again I'm proud you're my son! Don't let me down. Tell your teacher and all your friends hello for me. I miss you but soon we'll be together again. The time will pass soon.

Good night son and may God bless you and look after you. It's lonesome without you.

I love you,
Dad

First Lieutenant William P. Babcock *sent the following letter to Jack Whitford, his college classmate and best friend. It was written about a month after the Cambodian invasion in 1970 and after he left the field for a job as Civil Affairs officer. He served in Vietnam August 1969 to August 1970 as an Infantry platoon leader of 25 to 35 men in the jungles of the Central Highlands in II Corps. His honors include the Silver Star and the Purple Heart. Lieutenant Babcock now serves as Colonel and Deputy Chief of Staff of Operations for the Rhode Island National Guard.*

23 June 1970

Dear Jack,

I read in the *Times* about your father's wife, Ray. It was quite a shock. I imagine it was for everyone.

I finally got my job in the rear and won't have to go back to the field again. I'm the battalion S-5. The S-5 is the civil affairs officer. I work with the Vietnamese people, trying to help them any way I can. Right now we are helping one hamlet fix up a school. We also give them medical aid for minor things such as cuts, burns, sores, and bruises. Some days we treat as many as 200 people, mostly little kids under four years old.

Did I tell you that I got a silver star for our little party in Cambodia? Your friend, the hero! I suppose some people back home would call me a war mongering murdering imperialist, but actually I won the SS for saving lives, not for taking them.

Only 38 days left now. Time seems to go quickly at times but other days it just seems to drag by. Can't wait till I'm back to that old dull routine of making the rounds with all the other drunks.

See you soon,
Your Brother,
Bill

*The next letter was sent to Lieutenant Babcock's girlfriend at the time, Evelyn Dwyer (now Johnson).*

3 May 1970

Dear Ev,

We were supposed to leave on our new mission but something came up and the whole mission was canceled. We don't know why yet. In fact no one seems to know anything yet. All we have been told so far is that "all future operations will be to the west." The question is, how *far to the west?* As you can see by looking at a map, Cambodia is to the west. Everyone is a little nervous to say the least. It's really a farfetched idea that we would go to Cambodia but it is possible. It is even more possible that we move to a place near the border. You'll remember we weren't too far from Cambodia last December. LZ Lynn was only eight klicks from the border.

I should know by this afternoon what is going on. At least I hope I do. It probably won't be any big thing after all, but just not knowing has everyone wondering about Cambodia.

I'll let you know what happens, of course, but don't be surprised if the next letter is postmarked from Cambodia.

Love,
Bill

COMMANDER WILLIAM WILSON *of Massachusetts served with the U.S. Navy attached to the Naval Support Activity Saigon from November 1970 until November 1971, beginning as a 19-year-old third class petty officer. He was stationed on the YRBM-21 located on the Mekong River one kilometer from the Cambodian border. They were responsible for supporting Vietnamese and Cambodian river assault and providing direct support to convoys transiting to Phnom Penh via the Mekong. Commander Wilson repaired cryptographic equipment, radio receivers, and radars on the riverine crafts, and armed and refueled UH1-B Seawolves stationed on the YRBM-21. Joining the Naval Reserves upon his departure from active duty, he has had over 32 years of continuous naval service.*

*The following letters were included in his personal daily journal, intended to be read by his family at some point in the future.*

Day 88, 89, 90
February 10, 1971

Dear Dad,

Back at the YRBM-21 at last. I think if I were to stay in Nha Be for any length of time I would turn into some sort of degenerate. Like Bruce said when I left home, when you come home you'll be fucked up. You'll either be a pothead, alcoholic, or a sex maniac. I believe it's the truth. Out here on the border there isn't too much chance of that. Brownie going crazy at Nha Be.

Chambers has venereal warts. He's in rough shape in more ways than one. Brown tried to prove how animal he was by twisting the head of a monkey in one of the bars. This is what he says anyway.

Stopped at Long Xuyen on our way back from Saigon. Fixed wing to Long Xuyen and helo to the 21. At Long Xuyen, I watched some little kids using the solid propellant of some stockpiled rockets to play with. They would light it and watch it burn. Saigon sucked on this trip. Those people really stink. They're always trying to sell you stuff or have you bring them stuff for their black market,

154

or robbing you and just plain trying to put the screws to you. The VNs can have this fucking country. I don't know who would want it. I sure as hell don't!

Love,

Trip

Day 97

February 17, 1971

Dear Dad,

Was in my rack last night when I awakened by someone saying that Hong Ngu was overrun. I had just met those guys yesterday. I went up on the mess decks. It wasn't Hong Ngu but the PF output one klick from it. They brought the seven casualties down by skimmer. These guys were fucked up! They were riddled with holes and covered with blood. I helped carry one guy in on a stretcher. The doctor took one look at the guy and said he was dying. It was written all over his face. He was going fast. They started externally pumping his heart but he just lay there with his eyes wide open. They put a blanket over him a few minutes later. They worked on the other guys taking shrapnel out of them. Almost got sick once. There were bloody bandages and junk all over the place. The smell was awful. Another guy died a few minutes later. He was pretty well riddled up too. They put the dead guys out in the mess lines with a blanket over them. That made me think a bit as I passed them. A few minutes ago they were alive living thinking human beings, but now they were just a limp mass of blood and bones on a stretcher. They put the dead guys in body bags. It was like a big garbage bag. They hauled them up to the dust-off helo like a sack of potatoes. I don't know if the other five casualties made it or not. I don't think one guy did because there was a big pool of blood under his head.

Love,

Trip

Day 221–222
June 21–22, 1971

Dear Dad,

There is something wrong with the water and it's just killing everyone. Screaming yellow zonkers! Went to GQ the other night. The 9610 took a couple of mortars. Since we were so close we went to GQ too. I was sick to begin with. This isn't helping. The Seawolves went up and put a strike in. Pretty to watch! Today they held a surprise dope inspection. Of all the people to get caught, it was Davis. I didn't believe it. I guess with all the yelling back home about heroin freaks they are really cracking down. It's a good idea.

Love,
Trip

SERGEANT MAJOR RAYMOND EBBETS *served with the U.S. Army in 1972 and in Thailand in 1973. A graduate of a Vietnamese language class in Monterey, California, he returned to Vietnam in 1973 to work for ITT-FEC and was evacuated in April 1975. He married a Vietnamese woman that same month. He has been with the U.S. Army Reserve since 1983 and has had two deployments—to Haiti in 1995 and to Cambodia in 1996. He is currently an Army Reserve Sergeant Major. He wrote the following letter to his parents in Stockbridge, Massachusetts.*

20 Sep 72

Dear Mom and Dad,

Well, tomorrow it will be six mos. here, halfway. Time is almost going too fast. If we don't spend all our time here it will be somewhere else. But the word is we will be here until next March.

Let me know when you get the package. There are so many good things I could send home, but if I do I'll want one too, there is so much, jewelry, pottery, paintings, clothes, materials, a veritable wealth, and food, but that can't be brought home.

22 Sep is the Moon Festival in Cholon. It honors a man who was banished to the moon.

Also, mooncakes are sold all over town in Banh Trung Thu. They cost about 50–75 cents for one, expensive, and are filled with nuts and fruits.

Last break, Steve and me went to town shopping. He bought material for curtains and things for the house he and eight guys are living in. Some are on other tricks (shifts), so it's never crowded there. We bought some tom cang, or big crayfish about 5–6 inches long, 2.2 lbs. for 700P or ⅓ of $5.00, for now on I'll let you figure out what things cost. When you get used to another money system, it seems normal and you don't have to convert 2,350P for $5.00. We also bought two small heads of lettuce for 20P and 1.1 lb. of cooked Chinese noodles for 35P, pretty cheap.

That afternoon we cooked it, real good. On Cong Ly Street, the main road to Saigon, a new restaurant opened, open air. The food is good. They specialize in sauteed food and Banh Bao, these are really good, it's a steamed roll made of a cooked sweet dough, filled with different kinds of meats and veg. And one inch long duck egg. Really delicious, I'll bring a VN recipe book home and we'll eat good.

I can't say I'm sorry I joined the Army, it's been good, "not the army." Everyone from our class misses Monterey, perhaps more so than home, after all we know each other more than the guys back home. Besides, I only have a few friends back home and scattered all over. Two kids have even reupped to be back, but I want to go back as a civilian.

Everybody at work has been reading a book called *Tet* and making comparisons. I hope this war is over soon. These two gov'ts. are really stupid, willing to destroy each other for some stupid ideologies. And we here are caught in the middle. And our job is probably doing more to further it than anybody. All this was said by the CO in a commander's interview, so it's really not classified. We give direct support to commanders in the field by passing on intelligence. One General said battles may be won by the grunt in the field, but it was the 509th whose information won the battle. Our station handles 80% of all traffic in South East Asia, so you can imagine what passed thru everyday. If somebody wanted to hurt the war effort, all he has to do is slow up a message. There are stories of guys who were late in sending a message that was late and did cost some lives.

To give you an idea of how we get everything, I went to fix one tape (teletype) and looked at the page copy. It was about a flight from Danang to Clark, RP, the list of names of who was on board and ETA. The last three names were three guys who were in our class and were now on flight status, it was really surprising seeing it, so I had to show everybody. We can keep up on our classmates minute by minute. That message was sent while they were en route, so we knew where they were before anyone. Well enough of telling all about my job.

Next week people from our class start taking R&R. Joe goes first. Good old wishy washy Joe. First we tell him to go to HA [Hawaii], then his wife wants to go to CA [California]. Now he is going home, probably to see his mother. I don't think he is too excited, I think he'll miss his girlfriend. So many of the guys in our class, I really don't understand. Joe, for one, he really gets on everybody's nerves, a typical loud American. Another guy nothing but a slave to his "you know what," as Bill puts it. Bill says he wonders how they will feel for two wks being a one woman man. There should be interesting stories when they get back.

But Bill is funny, he is looking forward to HA [Hawaii]. Like he said his wife will know what he hasn't been doing when he gets there. Bill has such a way of putting things.

Well, hell, I just about wrote everything. Well until next letter.

Love,

Ray

When I started this letter, it was going to be short, because I couldn't think of anything to say, but it will probably be the longest letter of the year.

COMMANDER JAY PHELAN *was assigned as flight surgeon, Carrier Air Wing 11, based at Naval Air Station, Miramar, California, during his tour in Vietnam. He was deployed on the carrier USS* Kitty Hawk *twice during his tour, once from autumn 1970 to the summer of 1971, and again starting in February 1972. He was awarded an Air Medal in 1971. He resumed active duty in January 1993, serves as a flight surgeon and otolaryngologist, and supports NASA by serving as helicopter rescue doctor at shuttle launches and landings. Commander Phelan wrote the following letters to his then-girlfriend, now wife, Bonnie Gaye Brasfield, of San Diego, California. The first letter was written while he was a flight surgeon to both Air Wing F-4 Phantom squadrons, the Aardvarks (VF-114) and the Black Lions (VF-213). There was a gentle rivalry going on.*

May 22, 1972

Dear Bonnie,

On the tanker flight today we had to go 200 miles north to tank two F-4s who were patrolling around Haiphong. They were Black Lions. While tanking, I heard over the radio, "Is that you, Jay?" It was Skip Meinhold. Then, "When are you going to give me some pills? I've had the runs for a week." It was Andy Burgess. This was going out over the air and many people heard it. All I could say was, "Damn—see me when you get back." Then, as tanking was complete, Stanley Wyluda, Skip's RIO, said, "Thanks for the gas, traitor"—a reference to the orange aardvark on my helmet. The North Vietnamese must have wondered what types fly in Navy planes.

*The following letter was written to Bonnie while Commander Phelan was serving in the Gulf of Tonkin.*

March 21, 1972

Gulf of Tonkin

Dear Bonnie,

Duty tonight, and *already* I've been called down to see two suicide attempts with pills. I had duty on the 13th and had one—then none for three days. It was my duty the 17th and I had another (at 2:30 A.M.)—then none for three days. I have the duty again tonight and *two* before I even get to sleep. I hate it! The bastards may be unhappy, but they're also quite immature and are trying to manipulate me. I hate very much being manipulated, and find it hard to keep my cool when one of these kids comes in half flaked out. Each time one comes in now, I assess the situation, determine if he's in any danger, feel out his intentions, then either (1) pump his stomach unpleasantly, (2) chew his ass severely, (3) scare him with the seriousness of what he's done, or (rarely) (4) sympathize. No one is ecstatic about being on board ship, so these guys have a lot of company in their unhappiness. Why don't they all take pills? It may happen if others see these guys getting discharged for their attempts. But why not discharge them—who wants them around, anyhow? It's quite a dilemma, and no one has the answer. One thing is for sure, though. These guys will always have problems when things don't go their way, and probably won't handle themselves any better as civilians than they did in the Navy.

#56                    May 19
                       At sea
                       48 Days

Dear Bonnie,
        At last — a mail call and I
got your letter #64.  63 is still
out somewhere, but what the hell.
Today was a great day because I heard
from you. But no package from your
father, nothing from Connie or Crane,
and no orders! I did hear from my
Aunt + Uncle, who are trying to entice
me to visit them. I really think OH... LONESOME ME
I will after I leave you in Hawaii, If we get to
Hawaii. Ron approved my leave, but I already knew
he would. CAB and the Ship's XO still have to OK
it, and they are the only hurdle. PRAY out loud.
        I've enclosed a check for $20 to supplement the
one of $25 I sent before, for the phone bill. That
was quite a bill - could have nearly bought your
China.
        Bruce Menella said Louise would be meeting
him, I think, but not in Hawaii because there's
not enough time. I believe she came to Cubi. I may
be wrong - I might be thinking of Sue Halenza and
Danny Faherty's girl (who bought a three month
excursion to the Far East). I'll know when we
get there in 4 or 5 days. Wow! Solid land
under my feet! A couple of days to get some sun!
A couple of nights to get drunk! A couple of mornings
to regret!
        Is Sue Halenza really a lousy housekeeper?
As long as the place didn't have more crap tha—

*A letter from Commander Jay Phelan to his then-girlfriend
(now wife) Bonnie Brasfield.*

our house on Pendleton, I guess it's all right.

So Erna McKinney had another girl. What did you mean its easier to raise 3 girls than 2 girls and one boy? Are we that hard to raise? Anyhow, I think 3 kids are tough to raise no matter what they are.

We're still bombing the North, and when we do this we're usually located 35-50 miles off the North Vietnamese Coast

(This is a rough idea)

RED CHINA

Hanoi
Haiphong    Gulf of Tonkin
Thanh Hoa        Hainan (Red China)
North Viet Nam    Vinh        30 hours        →    CUBI
                    ← Carrier area north
                DMZ
LAOS
S. Viet Nam | Hue

Saigon

As you can see, we're right in the thick of it, but it looks more serious than it really is. No need to worry at all.

The picture I've drawn is just not right, but I don't know when I'll get another chance to work on it because Richard's usually here. I did your nose about 5 times without being satisfied. I'm sending it anyway because it represented a couple of hours work, the last hour hornier than hell. It is much more enjoyable to touch your breasts than draw them, because you are there, and we can feel each other's responses. But it won't be long. I love you —

Jay

*The following letter, dated April 14, 1972, and sent from the Gulf of Tonkin, mentions Pat Kellaway, the wife of the squadron's commanding officer (VF-114). Clemie McKinney and Joe Greenleaf, also mentioned in the letter, were later confirmed killed in action.*

Dear Bonnie,

If you've seen Pat Kellaway recently, you probably know that the squadron lost a plane this afternoon, and the two guys are now missing in action. It doesn't look good. The first I heard of it was from one of the corpsmen as I got out of surgery. I'm sure you don't know the guys, but you may know their wives—Clemie McKinney and Joe Greenleaf. I had just done Clemie's annual physical exam this morning. I'm sure it's shaken the rest of the squadron, although they say very little, as is the usual custom. I hope the wives you know don't get too upset, although I know it will have an effect on them. This is not last year's war.

# THE VIETNAMESE PEOPLE

*"These are a suppressed people fighting*
*for their freedom and the pursuit of happiness.*
*They have very little comforts*
*and fewer possessions."*

LIEUTENANT (JG) PINNEKER, *a Navy pilot in Attack Squadron 144, was killed on a mission in March 1966. The following letter was written by Captain Nguyen-Van-Tien to his widow, expressing the heartfelt appreciation of the Vietnamese people for American sacrifices in their struggle for independence. Lieutenant Pinneker's Commanding Officer, D. B. Miller, notes that after the memorial services referred to in the letter, over one hundred local townspeople stayed on to ask the local Army Advisor if there were anything they could do for the pilot's family.*

Hoa Dong, on 30th March 1966

Dear Mrs. Pinneker,

This letter should reach you immediately after the tragic news of your husband's death. I have purposely allowed enough time to pass to permit the U.S. officials to perform their procedure of notification of next of kin, and to allow you a few days to recover yourself.

I am a Vietnamese Army Captain, District Chief of Hoa Dong, Gocong Province and my name is Nguyen-Van-Tien. Hoa Dong is situated some thirty miles southwest of Saigon.

Lieutenant Pinneker was killed in the coconut grove two miles southwest of my district town while piloting his plane in a strike against a Viet Cong Company.

Writing on behalf of the entire Vietnamese community in Hoa Dong, I would like to express our most sincere condolences to all those mourning the death of your brave husband.

We did not know your husband by sight, but the name Pinneker will always be present in our minds. He died according to God's will, but his memory continues to live sharply with us.

As the people of Hoa Dong watched, he intrepidly carried out his mission over our area. We will always remember the way he made the supreme sacrifice in the manner of a true hero. We grieve deeply at the loss of one comrade in arms who fought so valiantly to preserve the freedom of the Vietnamese people.

To us, the death of Lieutenant Pinneker is highly significant. It brings to mind the daily sacrifice of the American youth in one country and is a brilliant example of self-abnegation that can only be found in those who still believe in a human brotherhood based on a common belief in Freedom, Democracy, and human Dignity.

In his memory, the people of Hoa Dong held religious memorial services (pictures of which are included) in the Pagoda and the Catholic Church on March 26th and March 27th respectively. These services were attended by hundreds of people who wanted to show in some way their appreciation for your husband's sacrifice.

Once again, united with you in mourning, we ardently pray that God rest his soul and that you please accept our sentiments of deepest regret and sincere gratitude.

Dai-ny Nguyen-Van-Tien

District Chief of Hoa-Dong

Gocong Vietnam

*In this series of letters written to his wife and family in North
Weymouth, Massachusetts,* WILLIAM P. TWIGGS, *a Navy man, offers
some insights into the plight of the Vietnamese people.*

Tuesday, May 17, 1966

Cam Ranh Bay

My dearest Rose, Deb, and family,

. . . I just want you to know how very proud I am of my family,
and of what you said in your letter about all of us over here. I just
couldn't help showing it to some of my very close buddies, and they
complimented me on my beautiful wife and darling daughter, and
your way of thinking. What you said is all true. If more people realized that these people over here have been fighting for their freedom
for over 35 years, and that they really look up to us guys over here,
because to them we represent the freedom they want so badly. And
the innocent people, especially the children that are hurt, killed, and
left homeless, really tears you apart, and you swear to God that you
will (as does everyone here) give these people their freedom, no matter what the cost. Like you said, we take our freedom for granted,
and we have never had our homes and cities and states bombed or
invaded by unfriendly forces who take anything they want and then
kill just for the sake of it.

I tell you . . . since I have been here I have seen some sights that
make you sick, but I won't go into it. I just wanted you to know that
us guys over here (be they Air Force, Army, Marines, or Navy) have
made a solemn promise: that for freedom we over here would not
balk at giving our lives, as so many have already done, and countless
more will . . . before we accomplish what we set out to do.

The reason I am writing a letter like this is not to worry you, but
to give you an idea of what could happen. Because every patrol I go
on—or, for that matter, all of us go on—our chances grow slimmer.
It's just like a poker hand; no matter how high a hand you draw,
someone holds a better one. . . .

May 20, 1966

. . . It is a real interesting country and a beautiful one, but the poor people are so mixed up. The Viet Cong tell them we will kill the husbands and children and enslave the women and girls, and then when we pull into a hamlet or village, the people are scared of us until we show and prove to them that we mean them no harm, which sometimes takes two days or two weeks or sometimes a month. But, believe me, it is worth the effort. When you see the gleam in their eyes and the tears, when our medics help some child or adult, or when we give them powdered milk, eggs, and of course rice. Maybe they don't come at once, but when you win their child's affection, you win theirs, also. So you can see how not just my time but everyone's time in our group is really taken up. But we have no gripes, because when we win them over, we defeat Charlie the Viet Cong, because he doesn't keep any promises he makes, and the villagers will turn him in to us. . . .

May 23, 1966

. . . We have a lot to be thankful for. It is sure funny how we take everything for granted, and how you never give it a second thought until you are in a place like this, and you see with your own eyes people starving and literally just giving up life. You pray to God and thank Him that you and your family don't have to suffer like these poor people do. I don't know, maybe I am just an old softy, but it just breaks your heart to see these people, especially the children, going hungry.

So that is why we men here have taken on the extra work of organizing this orphanage. At least we know that some children will have a place to sleep and three hot meals a day. We even have mothers who bring their children here because they know that they will be cared for. We even have a Philippine doctor who comes twice a week to take care of the sick and injured, and our own corpsman (a first class) is on hand at all times. We now have 73 young ones with us, ranging from two years to 13 years of age, and we are expecting more to come. Right now we put them up in tents. The orphanage is about 16 miles away in a fairly safe area. The ROK Marines [Republic of Korea] look after it for us when we cannot be there. . . .

May 31, 1966

. . . A job is a job, although this is a hell of a place to be. But after this hitch or tour is over, we can be together again . . . and I will have the satisfaction of knowing that I did my part. . . .

June 27, 1966

. . . You know, it's funny, when I am a guard at night—just you and your thoughts—I always catch myself drifting back and thinking of you and Deb, and just how dear you both are to me. I thank God that I have a family, especially like mine, and also thank Him for keeping my loved ones out of this holy mess. But it also makes you feel proud, especially when you walk into a village and the people say "You number one," which means the best there is, and they will share their last piece of food with you. And at night we have a serenade, which is the jungle noises: the birds, cats, and all types of weird sounds, but put together they sound kind of nice.

Love and Kisses,
Bill

PHILLIP N. LEGG *was an executive officer with AID, the federal government's Agency for International Development. Stationed in Region 2, Nha Trang Province, Legg described the operations of the agency in this letter to his wife in Arlington, Virginia.*

Dear Evelyn,

. . . You ask exactly what we do. . . .

To put it into a few words, our Provincial Representatives are out in the field serving as members of three-man teams, consisting of the Governor or Province Chief who is a military, a U.S. military Adviser and the Prov Rep. This team collaborates on every phase of province activity, including combat operations against the Viet Cong.

When the situation is right, pacification of a VC area starts and the team goes into action. The Province Chief and the military Adviser conduct the military operation and the USAID Prov Rep provides the necessary basic commodities to look after the women, children, and old people after the fight is over, or often as not, while it is still going on. . . .

In a nutshell, the Prov Reps bring hope to poor abused souls who have lost hope, home, family—particularly fathers and brothers—to the VC and have no one or place to turn. If they were left in this state, when our people withdraw they are *[sic]* sitting ducks for more VC propaganda. . . .

You can draw a parallel between this situation and our West in the early days. At first, the bad men could walk in like the VC and terrorize a town, and the timid folk would knuckle under. After law enforcement and the U.S. Cavalry arrived on the scene and bolstered the courage of the people, they rose up and threw the villains out of town.

That is what we are doing here.

We are inspiring confidence and respect in the people so that they will have the courage to resist VC recruitment of their young men, their food, their homes, their money, etc.

We are building schools, hospitals, marketplaces, vegetable land, and all with piasters which have been generated by the gigantic commodity import program which constitutes the bulk and 80 percent of our AID program in Vietnam. In other words, we are using counterpart funds but the budget is $150 million worth of piasters, plus 10 million in U.S. dollars.

This is a big thing, but the military effort would be completely wasted without it. . . .

*In a letter written home to his mother in Independence, Missouri,* EMIL SPADAFORA *of Advisory Team 99 spoke of American involvement in terms of the people of South Vietnam.*

13 August 1965
Duc Hoa, Vietnam

Dear Mom,

. . . Well time is sure flying for me. August is half over and another payday only two weeks away. I'll keep those checks coming as they are. When I get home I may buy a car or a small boat for skiing. I got to dream up something to use this money for. It's the only relaxing thought one has over here. . . .

Before I close I want to say one thing. If by chance something happens to me while I am over here, I don't want you to feel bitter about me having had to come in the first place. People in the U.S. don't realize what has happened or is happening over here. These are a suppressed people fighting for their freedom and pursuit of happiness. They have very little comforts and fewer possessions. They are glad, for the most part, to see us helping them. Our aid over here is not an obscure thing which makes one wonder who's getting rich off the U.S. You can see it in the small villages and jungle hamlets.

Duc Hoa now has a well for pure water built by Raymond Construction Company. When the Viet Cong mortared the village in July, it also rebuilt many homes. Bau Tri has an agriculture library for the people there—and so it goes. This is a war which must be fought here and now. The U.S. has been involved since 1961. These people have fought for *15 years.* They are tired. We are more or less a fresh start for them. We are fighting communism, which cannot be allowed to spread. If we leave Vietnam it will only delay the war to another time and place. Next we would be fighting on home soil. It makes me sick to hear of the demonstrations in the U.S. about Vietnam. These people are misinformed or pro-communists or just plain fools. I am proud to be serving here and will always feel I did my part for freedom's cause. If something does happen to me I want you to feel as though there was a reason, which there is. I will have died for freedom and my beliefs. Is there a more noble cause?

Love,

Emil

*The story of Emil Spadafora's involvement with the South Vietnamese people is told in the following two letters. Because of her age, and because she is a widow, Mrs. Spadafora could not legally adopt the little orphan boy Ti; but her son placed the boy in a boarding school, and Mrs. Spadafora accepted the responsibility for his education and support until he was able to care for himself.*

18 April 1966

Cau Tram, Vietnam

Dear Mom,

Well here it is the 18th day of April and as they say over here, I'm getting real short! My health is holding up real fine and now, of all times, I am really used to this way of life!

As usual with my letters, I have a bit of a problem that needs much thought on your part. I've spent three months thinking on it and have finally reached a conclusion and now it is strictly up to you; without you there can be no solution. . . .

Three months ago a town called Cho Heip came under heavy attack during the night and we went to reinforce them. The town was defended by a small group of Popular Forces soldiers (like our National Guard) and, as fate had it, we were too late to save them. The VC killed all of them.

Our battalion managed to retake the town by daybreak. When we moved in only one person was left alive in the place: a small boy who was badly wounded. We took him to the American field hospital and after four or five weeks he was back on his feet, and one day he showed up here at the 1st/46th. His father was one of the soldiers at Cho Heip and was killed along with his mother. He came to me and, as usual, I couldn't refuse to help him. He has lived with me and stayed with me for the past three months, and we have become very attached to each other. The problem is, I don't want to leave him! There are thousands of war orphans over here and if he stays here, he will end up God knows where! This leaves one alternative. Bring him to the United States.

I can imagine your feelings about now and I fully realize the problems involved and the involvement on your part. It means raising another son, plus the fact that he will have many other problems Mike and I don't have. True he is Vietnamese, but he doesn't have a real Oriental appearance. (Even if he did I wouldn't care, but as it happens he doesn't, and this is the first thing people remark about when they see him.) He is 12 years old and has some education. He is very intelligent compared to an American 12-year-old, and picks up English fairly well. I went to a priest in Saigon and he tells me he will be of any help in the event you decide to accept him. He advised putting him in a Catholic school for the first two or three years so the Sisters can work with him and teach him English. This seems to be a very *big* barrier: ENGLISH. The boy is Catholic, so this will be a tremendous help. His name is Ti (pronounced Tea). I know for you this is a big decision to make. You are thinking of the problems involved with your trying to work and take care of him. The money involved, and of Mike and me. My only argument is this: Mike and I are set for life in many respects, due to the GI Bill which applies to him as well. We both are able to go to college and from there we can make our way. Mike and I need very little in the way of support. This boy has *nothing* and his future holds nothing for him over here. He will not have a chance in life. Even if he finishes high school in the States he will be *fifty* times better off than he would here. I realize I can't help *all* the orphans in the world and wouldn't attempt to, but I can help *one* and I *want* to. The priest in Saigon has spent many hours talking to me about this and has posed many questions about future problems. He has thoroughly acquainted me with the "con" side, and after much thought, I am *sure* I want him to come home with me.

I want you to go and see a priest and show him this letter, *talk* with him and then decide. Time is important, but not too pressing as of yet. Let me know in the next 30 days or so. I may stay here an extra month or so if you decide to take him for two reasons. First I want to be with him when he comes, and second I can be with him for my 30-day leave and *everything* won't be strange to him. He can get to know *you* through me. My little knowledge of Vietnamese will help. H. Blieberger, my Asst. Senior Adviser, is writing you a letter since he is also a war orphan from Germany. He is familiar with the problems Ti will encounter and can clarify some of your doubts, which I'm sure you have. Since I'm not married, you must sign the adoption papers, but you will have all the monetary assistance and help from me I can muster. In short, I love and want to help this boy. I only hope and *pray* you see fit to take him.

Love,
Emil

April 30, 1966
Duc Hoa

Dear Mom,

Well here we are in Duc Hoa again but only for a few days. We will return to Cau Tram about Wednesday or Thursday. Since we've been here we haven't had any mail, so when we do go back I am looking forward to getting *a letter from home.*

The reason for this letter isn't just to let you know I'm okay. I put in for a *six* months extension last week. I asked to be extended to a Vietnamese Ranger Battalion. If there are no openings available with the Rangers I will probably come home, but if there are, I won't be home until December. I know what you're thinking about now: WHY!! My reasons are many but there are two main ones.

First of all is Ti. If I stay here longer I may be able to help him find a start over here, since I'm sure you won't take him. Second is because I believe so strongly in what I am doing over here.

I realize there are people who could take my place but they lack experience. I hate to waste my experience over here stateside. I'm still not sure whether the extension will be approved or not, so I can't say when I'll *definitely* be home. I'll keep you posted.

I won't elaborate any more on Ti because I feel your decision is already in the mail and you already know how *I* feel about him. I can't do anymore but *hope.* . . .

Well it's getting late so I'd better close for now. My love to all and take care of yourself.

Love,

Emil

*A Vietnamese officer's reaction to Emil Spadafora's efforts on behalf of the war orphan, Ti, are described by* MAJOR NGUYEN-TIEN-SUNG *in a letter to Mrs. Spadafora.*

March 7, 1966
Saigon

Dear Madam:

First, let me present myself to you. I'm a Vietnamese officer working closely with your son in the first battalion of 46 Regiment. He has been long time with us, but we could not have him for six months more. Sorry that he leaves us. You can be proud of your son, Madam, he is good friend in this unit. Every soldier knows him, appreciates his bravery in combat and his behavior. I had opportunity to help him in that he tried to do to Ti, a little orphan boy. I realize he loves Ti and understood his feelings. I have been happy to cooperate in that. He comes to see us, my wife and my children at home, and they are happy with his company.

He told me about you. . . . I don't know you, but I think I can imagine you through him—so I dare say you have helped my country in our fighting. Please pray God to shorten this war, Madam. Pray for having peace; we need this to reorganize our country.

I hope this first letter could be followed by others. . . . Please forgive me if my English is bad—I am just starting in it.

God bless you, Madam, and bring you good health.

Yours Sincerely,
Major Nguyen-Tien-Sung

BARBARA J. LILLY, *who served in Vietnam as a recreation worker with the American Red Cross, from March 1967 to March 1968 as a civilian, was part of the mobile program called Supplemental Recreational Activities Overseas, also known as the "Donut Dollies." The program was designed to reach out to the troops in the field who could not get back to the base camps, sometimes for months at a time. She sent the following letter to her parents, Leonard and Mary Dorr, who were living in Detroit, Michigan.*

*Barbara Lilly at a Roman Catholic orphanage, Vietnam, 1968
(photo taken by unknown photographer with Brenda's camera)*

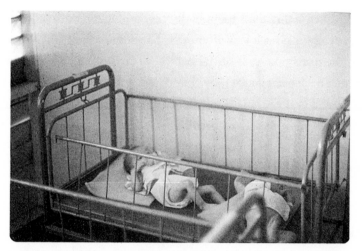

*Babies in a Vietnamese orphanage, 1968 (photo by Barbara Lilly)*

*Vietnamese children, 1968 (photo by Barbara Lilly)*

Tuesday, 5 November 1968
Cam Ranh Army

Sunday I went to an orphanage across the bay. I just couldn't believe the primitive conditions. The babies—about 12 under two or one months, and about seven under a year, were just pathetic. Some were real cute but all of them had sores and looked undernourished. They really need a lot of attention. The seven- and eight-year-olds help the nuns take care of the babies. There was one little girl who couldn't have been a foot long. I don't know how she's alive. The flies were awful and the smell, too. There was one baby boy who looked about two months old who could have been put in any American nursery and not been out of place. The nun—she spoke a little English—said his father comes to visit. He must be a GI. How sad. We're going to try to organize a work party to go over there and bathe the kids and take a medic and put medicine on the sores, etc. This one baby had little blisters all over her bottom and the "medicine" the nuns had was a can of baby powder. For blankets they use old Army towels and other scraps of material. The teeny "cribs" are slings a little off the floor, and the bigger babies sleep in cribs that are just metal with the little holes in it—no padding, no nothing. There's a man from a civilian corporation who built latrines and showers for them but their only source of water is a small well. And their outhouses are right over the well, so all their water is contaminated. It's really sad. I've already spoken to people about getting water trucks to go there, so maybe it will come through. As it is the showers, etc., are useless because the well can't furnish enough water. I hope we'll be able to get the place some help but there's always a problem as the Vietnamese won't always use what they're given. [For example,] mosquito nets, etc., as they say they make it too hot. We've got an interpreter lined up so we'll probably do all this early in December.

Sunday morning I went to a monastery near here called Myca Mission. The priest in charge invited us to join him for some rice wine. They make it here for a livelihood. Really good stuff! I couldn't go inside the chapel as I'm a female (in case you forgot) but the fellas I went with could.

RABBI RICHARD E. DRYER, *an Army chaplain, wrote the following letter to the National Jewish Welfare Board's Commission on Jewish Chaplaincy in 1965. (Reprinted by permission of the National Jewish Welfare Board.)*

Friday, October 1, 1965

Dear Sirs:

More and more American civilians are coming to Vietnam these days with preconceived ideas. They spend a few days here interviewing people, interviews intended primarily to strengthen and support their preconceived ideas. Then they return to the United States as self-proclaimed experts on the Vietnam situation.

I have lived for over seven months in this beautiful but embattled country. Since I have been the only rabbi available during this period to serve both the American Jewish servicemen and U.S. civilian aid officials, I have had the responsibility and the opportunity to travel the entire length and breadth of South Vietnam, from Quang Tri in the north to Ca Mau in the south, from the largest cities to the tiniest hamlets. I have had long conversations with many religious leaders, students, and ordinary people. All of them want peace in their country. But not one of them has said to me that he believes that a satisfactory peace could be obtained by the unilateral withdrawal of the American military forces.

I have been stopped by Vietnamese as I walked down the street in civilian clothes the day after a Viet Cong bombing of an American troop billet. These Vietnamese wanted to express their heartfelt and sincere grief—and thanks—to an American, any American. These ordinary people were deeply grateful for the presence of the American military in their country. Their own dead they could accept more easily than the sacrifices of men from thousands of miles away who were here to defend their freedom.

A refugee from North Vietnam invited me to his humble home to share a meal with him and his brother and their 10 children. He, too, stopped me on the street only because he recognized me as an American and wanted me to know how he felt. I accepted the invitation, and learned how his parents had been brutally murdered by the Viet Cong—not killed by the accidents of war, but brutally, deliberately murdered.

A taxi driver bought *me* a drink, simply because I was an American and I was in his country to protect him.

While the Viet Cong plunder and terrorize, rob and murder, what are the Americans doing to warrant the affection of the Vietnamese? They are acting like typical goodhearted Americans. For example, a Jewish Marine surgeon and a Protestant Marine chaplain have teamed up to adopt Catholic and Buddhist orphanages in their area. The chaplain takes up special offerings from his military congregation to buy medical and baby supplies, and the surgeon puts the money collected to good use.

I have had to counsel with an American serviceman who has been tortured by nightmares since the night the Viet Cong bombed a civilian restaurant in Saigon. This typically generous American had picked up a hungry five-year-old Vietnamese child and taken her to the restaurant for dinner. He came out of the bombing unhurt. She started to run away after the first bomb went off and was killed by the second.

Being truly liberal means to approach a subject with an open mind, to examine impartially both sides of a matter.

War is evil. There is no doubt about that. But the issues in Vietnam are not that simple. The United States is not opposed to negotiations; the Communists are. The United States did not start an aggressive war on the territory of another country; the Communists did. The United States has not engaged in deliberate terror against civilian populations; the Communists do. The United States has not deliberately kidnapped and murdered civilian women and children, teachers and communal leaders; the Communists have. The United States is not an uninvited foreign power on the territory of a peaceful country; the North Vietnamese are. It goes far beyond the demands of sensible liberalism to contend that American forces should withdraw from this war while the Communists continue to carry out their announced plans to subjugate South Vietnam.

I too was opposed to American involvement in the Vietnamese war—before I came over here. In fact, it took about four months before I became firmly convinced that we are doing the only thing we can do. I have tried to avoid hasty and ill-founded judgments. I have gained firsthand knowledge by being here for a long period of time and by talking with many Vietnamese in all sections of South Vietnam. I have heard of no refugees fleeing from us to the Communist-controlled portions of the country but I have seen thousands who have fled from them to us.

I certainly share the desire of all well-meaning people that this war be brought to an end as quickly as is reasonably possible. But we cannot bring this about unilaterally when we are not the aggressor, when the other side refuses even to consider a peaceful solution. For a time, we stopped the bombings of North Vietnam. This brought no cessation of Viet Cong aggression in the South. It only brought the response that no cease-fire would result from the cessation of the bombings unless this action was accompanied by a complete American withdrawal from Vietnam and a complete Communist takeover. I hate war as much as anyone, but this kind of submission is not an acceptable alternative.

Our present policy of continuing the military struggle is not a pleasant one, especially for those of us who are over here; but the prospect of giving in to a brutal, tyrannical aggressor is much less attractive. If pressure is to be brought, let it be applied to the side which refuses to consider any peaceful negotiations, not to the side that stands ever ready to consider any honorable proposal for peace.

Richard E. Dryer
Chaplain (Capt.) U.S. Army

Marine Captain Peter T. Duggan *tells of an incident which strengthened his convictions in the need to fight and that fed his hope for eventual victory.*

. . . I only knew him about six weeks; and of course there was the language barrier, and rank differences and Oriental reticence, but he became a friend anyway. At least he was my friend until he was murdered by the Viet Cong; now he is my cause. Mr. Tuong was the village chief of Hoa Lac village a few miles north of Da Nang. He was appointed to that job around the middle of January. He held it for five weeks. He was murdered. The facts of his death were in many newspapers. They were also covered quite well in an article in *Time* magazine. Briefly, he was machine-gunned by two Viet Cong while attending a Buddhist religious meeting in one of the hamlets in his village. Four other villagers were caught in the fire and killed as well. He was not even able to draw his pistol and defend himself. By the time Marines arrived he had been dead for 30 or 40 minutes. The Viet Cong escaped.

But his death is more significant than one more bitter little killing in a bitter little war. He was an effective chief. He was not a democrat. He probably could not have defined democracy or even have understood it. He was not elected to office. That was not practical. But he did understand his own people. He governed in a manner that was in keeping with Vietnamese tradition. He established a village council of elders to help him rule. Decisions were made at town meetings. The villagers were organized to help defend their area. Payments for work projects and relief supplies were distributed honestly. In short, he did his job. The more effective he became the more his life was in danger, yet he performed to the best of his ability. He helped the people, so the Viet Cong had to kill him. (That is the real horror of the antiwar demonstrations in the U.S. Those demonstrations sanction an organization that feels it must brutally murder anyone who is honestly helping the peasant.)

In his death, is there hope? I like to think so. People must be heartened by the picture of a poor but honest and brave man willing to risk his life to fight communism. If only there were more. Maybe, just maybe, there are more than we realize. When Mr. Tuong took over as village chief, the police chief in the village was an immature young man named Hung. Hung's main interests were reading movie magazines and chasing girls. Six weeks with Mr. Tuong changed all that. In six weeks he matured; he became a man. Tuong is dead but Hung is now village chief and is attempting to carry out his predecessor's program. He lacks experience, but by God is trying. He has seen what the Viet Cong can do and he is doing his best anyway. God rest Mr. Tuong; God help Mr. Hung. They both prove this lousy war can be won.

Capt. Peter T. Duggan, USMC

Da Nang

SEAMAN JOHN WINNIE *described his feelings about the death of a comrade and the Vietnamese people in a letter to his parents in Poughkeepsie, New York.*

Dear Mom and Dad,

I've worked when I could here on my BM-3 course. Not much time between unloading Marines and ammunition and ducking snipers.

They're as big and bad as Jersey mosquitoes are supposed to be. We're really going into this operation with both feet, tooth and nail.

Campbell got it this morning. Little Willie came close. His helmet deflected the bullet, but he got hit in the shoulder. He is out of commission now. It was a long trip upriver and every muscle aches from being so tense.

Sure miss Campbell . . . Willie. It still doesn't seem real. Usually, right now, we'd be sitting up on No. 5 hatch drinking coffee and shooting the breeze.

Suppose the kids are looking forward to Easter baskets and new outfits. Wish I could see them, but know they'll look nice.

*Six Days Later.*

Had a little excitement today while off-loading. Cramer was tied up alongside the salvage boat by the LCM ramp in the Sang Hue River. When the ramp was clear, Cramer took off to the ramp.

The current from his boat swamped and capsized two little boats that three Vietnamese boys were in. Engineer and signalman and I jumped in after them.

Poor kids were scared to death. We fished out their boat and paddles for them. They come around when we are anchored. They bum candy, cake, cigarettes from us. After smoking their cigarettes, I can understand their bumming ours.

Sometimes they bring out beer. Tastes like a combination of oil and turpentine. They're really a nice, friendly lot.

We felt so sorry for them when their boats got swamped. They are tiny people, and when their boats get swamped—with 28-ton boats you do that—you feel so big, awkward, and clumsy and a little ashamed.

But you can't help it. They race toward us when we're anchored off waiting to make the ramp.

I was playing cowboys and Indians with a five- or six-year-old after we landed. They're really cute.

Hey, be prepared for a growing mustache. Does it make me look older?

Still can't feel Campbell is gone—and Little Willie. Remember when you came to San Diego to say good-by? They were nice kids. Only Willie and I left out of five close buddies.

Well, will close. Hope mail goes out tomorrow. But it will soon be better seeing you all. My love to all. Write.

John

# REFLECTION

*"[A]fter you've been here, only as short a time as I have, your ideas change."*

*On February 1, 1966,* PRIVATE IST CLASS HIRAM D. STRICKLAND *was killed while on patrol near Bong Son, Vietnam. Almost a month after Pfc. Strickland's personal effects had been mailed home to his family in Graham, North Carolina, some of his buddies found a notebook beside his bed. It had been overlooked because it had fallen by the side of his tent. On the pad, in Pfc. Strickland's own handwriting, was the following letter.*

Dear Folks,

I'm writing this letter as my last one. You've probably already received word that I'm dead and that the government wishes to express its deepest regret.

Believe me, I didn't want to die, but I know it was my part of the job. I want my country to live for billions and billions of years to come.

I want it to stand as a light to all people oppressed and guide them to the same freedom we know. If we can stand and fight for freedom, then I think we have done the job God set down for us. It's up to every American to fight for the freedom we hold so dear. If we don't, the smells of free air could become dark and damp as in a prison cell.

We won't be able to look at ourselves in a mirror, much less at our sons and daughters, because we know we have failed our God, country, and our future generations.

I can hold my head high because I fought, whether it be in heaven or hell. Besides, the saying goes, "One more GI from Vietnam, St. Peter; I've served my time in hell."

I fought for Sandy, Nell, Gale [his sisters], Mom, and Dad. But when the twins and Sandy's kids get old enough, they'll probably have to fight, too. Tell them to go proudly and without fear of death because it is worth keeping the land free.

I remember a story from Mr. Williams' [Thomas Williams, a

teacher at Strickland's high school] English classes when I was a freshman that said, "The cowards die a thousand times, the brave die but once."

Don't mourn me, Mother, for I'm happy I died fighting my country's enemies, and I will live forever in people's minds. I've done what I've always dreamed of. Don't mourn me, for I died a soldier of the United States of America.

God bless you all and take care. I'll be seeing you in heaven.

Your loving son and brother,

Butch

COLONEL JAMES B. LINCOLN *served two tours in Vietnam, from March 1965 to October 1966, and again from November 1971 to November 1972. He served as an advisor to the South Vietnamese Army and company commander of an artillery battery in the 1st Infantry Division, U.S. Army. He was the first American in the area where he served in 1965, and the last American in the area in 1972. Having attended Vietnamese language school before each tour, he also served as an interpreter. His honors include the Combat Infantry Badge and the Vietnamese Cross of Gallantry.*

*The following letter was written to his brother, Clark.*

*Colonel James Lincoln with Vietnamese officer, giving out medicine in a local watch tower, 1965 (photographer unknown)*

14 Aug. 65

Dear Clark,

Receiving your letter today reminded me that I have never really written you a good letter about the state of things over here, from my point of view. Since your CO is using some of the info. in my letter as poop for TI classes, I had better give you the straight

195

word. First of all, I really did not intend for some of the things in my previous letters to be made "public," and you must be very careful what you say. Some of the GIs will write home about some of the things I said maybe, and they might be a little shaded—I think you see what I mean. Let me first answer some of your questions. When I said that many of the advisors over here were not very conscientious, I was speaking of the guys that work at the larger compounds and in Saigon, where many Americans are all together, and don't really have much contact with the Vietnamese or VC. There are only a few advisors that are really in the field—those are the unit advisors and the District advisors, like me. I would guess they number not many more than a couple thousand, out of the many thousands over here. This is a point to remember. I was referring mostly to the cowboy advisors, who carry very large pistols, but who only stay in a nice secure compound or office and once in a while take a chopper ride to some fairly remote area. The large combat operation I spoke of is a very common occurrence. I would say that less than ⅓ of all planned operations made any contact with the VC. There are various reasons—first, the VC have their own very efficient intelligence nets. There are probably VC sympathizers in every major Hq. of the Vietnam Army. There is usually at least a 24-hour planning period before any operation kicks off. This gives a lot of time for the plan to leak out, and it quite often does. All operations are planned by the VN [Vietnamese] officers, with the Americans looking over their shoulders offering advice. The Americans have one positive control over these operations—the choppers are all strictly American controlled, so we can always say the choppers are not available, if we do not go along with the plan. Almost all operations in the Delta involve airlifted troops, if they involve Battalions, so we do have a certain amount of control. However, in the other areas of the country, choppers are not used as much because of the jungle terrain, lack of good landing sites. Most of the time, however, even if we do not particularly like the VN plan, we will always provide the choppers. I have become a little more wise, since I wrote that letter about that operation that failed to kill a single VC. There are political reasons for some of the operations—the Gov. is just showing the people that they are being protected and supported by the Gov., more or less a show of force to help in winning the people over to the South VN Government. Next, the VC are extremely good at slipping out of an area, or hiding in an area where there is an operation. An example—near my area four Battalions entered an area to look for a VC company that was reported in the area. There was not a shot fired, and nobody could figure out how the VC slipped out of the area, all escape routes were covered with blocking positions. About a week later they went back into the same area and found out why. The VC had a fantastic underground network of caves to hit the entire Company, and all the entrances were next to impossible to find. (The caves were later destroyed with a napalm air strike.) You ask about the vulnerability or my location. Everywhere is vulnerable—if the VC want to make an attack, they have the upper hand. We can only fight them as best we can and wait for help to arrive. However, they always plan and execute very carefully. There is usually only one or two roads or entrances into an area they plan to attack. Quite often they will drop a few mortar rounds into a location, with no intention of making a ground attack. They realize, however, that the camp under attack will call for reinforcements, and they will come by truck since it will be nighttime. The main VC force simply waits along the road into the area and ambushes the relief force—it's all very simple. As soon as you think you have them figured out, they *will* make a ground attack, but so sorry you told the relief forces not to come because of suspected ambush. Another thing that has amazed me is the accuracy of the mortar. It is very difficult for them to carry the ammo., so it is precious and every round much counts. In almost all cases where they have mortared a location, all rounds hit right on target, including the first round. I guess they have one of their boys pace off the distance beforehand. I would say that the most that would ever happen to our town here is a mortaring—we are too close to a great deal of help. The VC can harass other more remote areas and not worry about help arriving in time to do any good.

Now I will give you a few points that I think will be interesting. First the Army of South VN itself. How good are the soldiers, are they well trained, etc. The soldiers themselves are good fighters, but they are very underpaid, and poorly led. A VN Sgt. makes about $30 a month, and the Battalion Cmdr., a Capt., makes only $80. Their morale is poor, and this brings about the biggest problem in the Army—AWOLs and deserters. The TO&E strength of a VN Inf. Bn. is 790 men, but the average present for duty strength is usually less than 400! This is true all over the country, and caused by deserters and AWOLs. The Gov. just doesn't look after their soldiers well enough to keep them happy. All soldiers' housing is terrible, dependents are not thought of in the least—they have no provisions for getting pay home when the husband is off on a big operation, maybe for over a month. There are many, many other problems that cause problems for the Army. However, many gains have been made because of the American advisors present at all levels of the Army, but they are very slow and a long time in coming. Next—poor leadership. The commanders of the Army units are usually inexperienced, and only worried about staying alive, and getting a soft job back in Saigon somewhere. The high level commanders are more worried about political things than military considerations. District chiefs are the same way—they usually plan and go out on as few operations as possible, mostly worried about keeping the province chief happy from a political viewpoint. Of course this can be partially justified because of the bad political situation throughout the country. Nobody is really sure who to support—maybe tomorrow there will be another coup and the guy they supported will be thrown out. It's all highly confusing, but one thing is sure—it really hurts the military effort. There are few good military leaders, and their units do real fine against the VC, but the majority are on the other side. I guess that's enough military poop for now. If you or your men know any specific questions, let me know.

I guess you know that Pat finally made the grade and is a Lt. in the AF and about to go to flight school—he is very anxious to get in the fight over here and for his sake I hope he makes it. Mary C. will be married on Dec. 4 to a guy I met in Frisco before I came over here. I think it is the best thing for her—she is a rather confused and unsure type now, and marriage should help her. Uncle Bub and Aunt C. met the future brother-in-law and everything is hunky-dory. I'm sure you know Bernie is now married, about to make Maj. And going to West Point to teach one of the six languages he knows. By the way, I think I told you that I ran into Tom Godfrey at Ft. Sill—he's a Lt., married, and now at flight school. We stared at each other one night in the O Club—we both knew each other but couldn't quite see the light. It was a real surprise.

I'm enclosing some news briefs that should be interesting, and a little VC propaganda, we capture a lot of propaganda like this. Also enclosing some info. on the mutual funds. The best thing to do would be to write the man who handles my funds for me, and let him give you a rundown. His address: Col. John P. Crehan, 3241 NW 20th S., Oklahoma City, 7, Okla. I think funds are a good bet now—the economy is booming because of the military situation. I put $100 every month in one fund, and $300 a year in the other. I am enclosing a recent letter from Col. Crehan, which is all I can find right now—I thought I had some brochures, but I can't find them. A couple pictures also—some of them aren't too good but read on the back, I describe.

Please save all this stuff carefully, and send it to the folks when you are finished, or keep it and bring it back with you—by the way, how much longer do you have over there? How about a picture of you and Jan—it's been a long time.

Well, I guess I have outdone myself with all this, so I'd better close.

Love to you both,

Jim

SPECIALIST 5TH CLASS BILL MCCLOUD *wrote the following letter to his parents, Bill and Joyce McCloud, of Ponca City, Oklahoma, and later noted that this was possibly the only time he did not capitalize his name.*

9 Jun 68

Sun. eve.

Day 76

Dear Mom and Dad,

I was listening to the radio two days ago when they first announced Bobby Kennedy had died from his bullet wounds. It was a very sad day; there were as many tears here as anywhere else in the world, and I'm not sure I want to come home.

It's kind of funny, but the last three weeks I have been reading everything I could get my hands on about him, and I was fast becoming a big fan of his.

For a man over here to be wounded or killed is expected and nothing much is said about it! But, he was a man that did not deserve the pain he received from the wounds, not to mention the pain his family is now bearing.

Betty's latest letter said her Grandma Hunt died of a heart attack. I don't mind being in a foreign country or fighting in the army, but I do mind being away from my family and the others I love when problems or bad times arise.

Love to all,

billy

*Specialist McCloud wrote the following letter to his mother, reflecting on the antiwar demonstrations and subsequent riots in Chicago in 1968.*

23 Sep 68

Mon. Aft

Day 182

Dear Mom,

It's almost 1:00 Monday afternoon and I am working. Nothing interesting has happened here the past few days.

Let me say a little more about the incident with the Chicago police. Even if the majority of the people involved were hostile demonstrators, which apparently they were not by any means, it still would not have justified their actions. By "their," I mean the police. Most of the guys over here, myself included, feel that people have a right to demonstrate to show they are against this war. The only thing I disapprove of is when they raise and carry a Viet Cong flag. Something should be done about those few. But, even if a girl was lowering the U.S. flag and raising a VC flag, that would still be no reason for a group of men to attack her with sticks. Oh, well.

Love,

Billy

SERGEANT GREG MOODY *served in the 3/12 3rd Marine Division for a year and a half in Vietnam. His honors include the Vietnam Campaign medal with device and the Vietnam Service medal with star. Sergeant Moody wrote the following letter home to his pastor, Dr. James L. Pleitz, of Florida, while on tour in Vietnam.*

*Sergeant Greg Moody, 1967 (photographed at USMC Recruit Depot, Paris Island, South Carolina)*

22 May 1968
Wed.

Dear Mr. Pleitz,

Today I received some literature from the church and I would like to thank you and the church for sending it as I like to know what the church is doing.

I would like to say at this time, that since I've arrived here in Viet Nam, I have learned much. As I travel from Dong Ha, where I am stationed, to Quang Tri, I am able to see the people and the effect of the war here on these people. These people have the look of weariness and of lost hope for peace. Death and fear are their constant companions. I thank God that my Mother and Dad and all my brothers and sisters do not have to worry each day about where their next meal will come from or which day will be their last because of a war that is all around them and which even comes into their own village. My generation and my parents' generation have been fortunate in that they have not known the horrible realities of war in their own country.

The Americans have taken for granted their wonderful freedom, which is a dream to the Vietnamese people here. With God's willingness and his protection, when I return home I will treasure my freedom I have been blessed with along with the Lord's mercy and kindness he has bestowed upon our Nation.

I will close for now knowing that God is watching over me and thankful to you for your teachings.

Sincerely yours,

Greg

P.S. Would like you to explain passage in Bible, in Jeremiah 20 verse 2, I believe? It has to do with the ways of the heathen. Would appreciate your help very much.

*Greg Moody's safe-conduct pass*

SPECIALIST JOHN A. FOSLAND *served with the U.S. Army, 101st Airborne Division and worked the Cambodian border as an infantryman. He received the Army Commendation Medal, Medal with V device, and Bronze Star. A life member of the Veterans of Foreign Wars, of which he has been the quartermaster for 30 years, he is also a 30-year member of the American Legion, and from 1970 to 1973 actively worked on the local and state level for the POW-MIA effort. He wrote 60 letters to his female pen pal, Carol Jackson of Tucson, Arizona, from December 1968 to July of 1969. He received her name in a Christmas package that she had sent to "any line soldier," and he started writing immediately.*

18 July 69

My Dear Carol,

Today I wrote you a letter and I didn't finish it. I feel empty tonight, and I want to hold someone very, very desperately. You see, at 10:00 A.M., at the time I was finishing your letter, the radios started bringing bad news. A very close friend of mine who I went into the Army with, whose name was always next to mine on a roster, who saved my life and kept me going when I said I'd quit, died today in this damn country. He had only 42 days left here and wanted to go home so bad. He lived about 70 miles from my home in the states, and I know his family well. He stood 6-4 and his name described him well—"FOREMAN." He carried the "big gun" when he first got here and handled it like a razor shaving a balloon. And when he talked with the gun, people followed.

There were six of us who said "I do" in that small, stale room before walking to the train taking us to learn about war. We called ourselves "The Dirty ½ Dozen." With 42 days left for each of us, we lost a real friend that seems to make this war worthless. The odd thing, I feel no hate or revenge. You might say a feeling of complete disgust or agony at the thought, "But why him?" He had such a will to get ahead in this losing world, Carol. I hope you never have to see a grown man cry. It's not a pretty sight seeing five people let the life drain out of them as the news filters through their fogged minds. Those people would have loved to be in his place. All that mature intelligence just went to waste.

I feel like I did when my father died. NOTHING! Nobody was around then it seemed either, but everyone was.

Carol, I'm lonely and everybody is around and cares. I believe I'm a bit crazy. Tonight I'm full of love and one of my best and reliable friends is waiting to go home because of what seems to be the unnecessary.

God help the men on line.

My love, Carol,

John

CAPTAIN MARSHALL A. HANSON *served two periods in Vietnam. He was aboard a 1st Class Midshipman Cruise while still in NROTC for six weeks from August to September 1971, then recommissioned from October 1972 to May 1973 and served aboard the USS* Niagara Falls, *which was awarded a Meritorious Unit Citation. He is now the Director of Legislation for the 22,500 member Naval Reserve Association and an active drilling reservist teaching leadership courses.*

*Captain Hanson wrote the following poem while a 22-year-old ensign with seven months experience on board the* Niagara Falls. *The U.S. Navy has a tradition that the officer of the deck of the first watch of the New Year—mid-watch: midnight to 4:00* A.M.—*write a poem rather than the normal deck log entry for a United States ship. Captain Hanson swapped watches to get the chance to write it.*

USS *Niagara Falls* (AFS-3) Zone Description: -8H
Date: Monday 1 Jan. 1973
At: Subic Bay, Republic of Philippines.


00:00–04:00
Pvt. Francis X McGraw,
On the far side of NSD.
How come you to gain such immortality?


You're not alone, Francis X.
Subic Bay holds many a famous name,
At least for the crews that man them.
Each sits at momentary Peace, waiting out the morrow.


Some are moored to the port.
Others to starboard like us.
All doubled up, fore and aft, secure.
Manned only with basics so the rest can escape for the night.

If only all could have off.
Wasn't that once a personal wish, McGraw?
Those nights you had the duty
But some must remain, just in case.

We are Yoked, under ready four.
Standing watch, as we must.
All is seemingly secured.
Thus time lapse slowly by, from thought to thought.

But, Francis X.
It takes just a second to change a year
There COMUSNAVPHIL has no command.
With another second could come that decision for peace,
Then home, for all.

SPECIALIST 5TH CLASS PAUL CAMERON *served as light weapons infantryman, duty soldier, security guard, and administrative specialist. The first half of his 365-day tour was with the 1st Infantry Division, 11 Bravo, at Di An, South Vietnam, as light weapons infantryman and then duty soldier assigned to 1st Administration Company. His honors include the National Defense Medal and the Vietnam Service Medal with two bronze stars.*

*He wrote the following letter to his wife, Cherri, who was expecting the birth of their first child in July 1970. It was written soon after the Kent State massacre on May 4, 1970.*

May 1970

Dear Cherri,

I hope this letter finds you and everything okay. I wish I could be there with you when the baby arrives. I figured it up the other day that our new arrival would be four months old when I get home.

We read about the awful Kent State killings by the National Guard. What the hell's going on? Has Nixon lost the rest of his mind? When I read about it, I thought to myself that we should have went ahead with our plans at Ft. Ord and joined our friends to Canada. Yes, I'm pretty upset over this criminal act by our own government. One of our tower guards, Mike, reacted with this comment when he read it, "Hey Nixon! Send us some of those M-16s you used at Kent State and we'll put them to use against Charlie!" Mike came from a line unit and knows all about M-16 defects over here. I was cleaning my M-16 earlier today and the firing pin was broken. My NCO told me to join the club and he would try to get it replaced.

According to what we read this happened on May 4th, your mom's birthday (tell her Happy Birthday for me) about a week ago. I don't know what the six o'clock evening news is reporting about this place, but believe me, we were in Cambodia and Laos long before Nixon gave his orders. I'm afraid he just accelerated the Cold War with Russia and dug us in deeper over here. So much for Vietnamization, which was supposed to bring all of us home soon.

One of our tower guards left to go home today and I've got to take his 12-hour shift. Got to run. Take care of you and that little guy or girl growing inside of your tummy. If you can remember, send me news clippings of the Kent State tragedy. I don't think the *Stars and Stripes* newspaper is telling us the whole story over here.

Love always,
Paul

*Specialist Cameron wrote the following letter to President Richard M. Nixon, Commander-in-Chief of the Armed Forces, in September 1970. He was due to leave Vietnam in November of 1970, six weeks away. Instead of orders to go home in November, he received orders for border patrol duty on the Russian/Czech border, with no leave time in between.*

September 1970

Dear Mr. President:

You will probably never see this letter, but I sure would like someone in Washington to consider my request and return a reply real soon.

I am finishing up my tour in Vietnam and scheduled to leave in November of this year. Today, I received orders for Czechoslovakia and assigned duties as a security border patrol guard. According to my orders, I will not be granted any leave time. I have an infant son who will be three months old and I've never seen him. My wife and I have not seen one another since my brief leave prior to me leaving for my Vietnam tour in November 1969.

Mr. President, I feel as though I have sacrificed enough for my country. Drafted at the age of 24, married, and teaching in a rural high school, I answered the call to serve my country. Leaving for

Vietnam was difficult, with my wife expecting our first born. However, I went and I've almost completed my tour.

Therefore, I wish to request orders for a stateside duty assignment to finish out my 24 month active service with the United States Army. I would appreciate an assignment as close to my home of Missouri as possible. In the event that my current orders cannot be changed, at least allow me some leave time between Vietnam and Czechoslovakia so I can be with my wife and infant son for a few days.

Thank you for your time and serious consideration regarding this request.

Sincerely yours,

SP5 Paul S. Cameron

US487520686

*Approximately three weeks later he received a letter of appreciation for his service in Vietnam and an apology regarding the first set of orders. He was given a new set of orders to report to Fort Leonard Wood, Missouri, after the Christmas holidays.*

*The following letter was written by* JEANNE WILLIAMS, *a volunteer with the International Voluntary Services, Inc., a private nonprofit organization founded in 1953 to help development in rural communities around the world. During the Vietnam War, IVS was supported by both the U.S. government and that of South Vietnam (which, under contract, paid the expenses of IVS workers in Vietnam). Most IVS personnel in Vietnam were recent college graduates with training in a field related to rural development and education. Volunteers wrote and sent their letters to the IVS headquarters in Washington, which distributed up to 100 copies to specified friends and relatives as a service to its workers.*

Qui Nhon, Vietnam
April 4, 1966

Dear Friends,

Qui Nhon, following the questionable example of the city of Hue (whey), closed its schools today until further notice. The political turmoil of the aforementioned city has spread to our town. We have seen demonstrations, assemblies of students and boycott of classes; and last evening a group of students tried unsuccessfully to seize the radio station. There was firing into the air and numerous arrests were made, among them some of my students. A hush surrounds Qui Nhon today, though perhaps a deceptive one. No demonstrations, no banner carrying. But Mr. Ai, director of the technical school, feels sure that meetings are going on in several places. Why all the disorder now? Students (or those who lead them . . . ?) are clamoring for a civilian government; they want Ky out, they say. They want less American influence on their officials, as they fear it is our desire to control their government. . . .

April 14

The question which more of you ask than any other is that concerning the proximity of "the war" to Qui Nhon. You indicate that, while the newspapers are full of war stories, I rarely dwell on this aspect of life in Vietnam. This is because, in reality, the war affects my living very little. We often hear mortaring, and sometimes bombing, which we know is about 15 to 20 miles away (no farther) and which is "friendly." Frequently we'll hear shots from within Qui Nhon, but we rarely learn the source or reason—usually a guard shooting at something that looked out of the ordinary. Because there is a lot of activity in our province (Binh Dinh), Qui Nhon, the largest town in the province, is always bustling: convoys of troop-laden trucks heading out of town or returning from an operation, planes continually landing or taking off, helicopters carrying out their indispensable duties. But we walk along the streets freely, ride our bicycles throughout Qui Nhon—further if we wish—and drive to many places in the province (some, of course, are definitely not safe).

The sight which really gives the term "Viet Cong" (or "Victor Charlie," as he's known) meaning to me is that of the patients at the civilian (or Province) Hospital. They come from far and near—by truck, by lambretta (tiny buses), by cyclo, by foot—90 percent of them bearing war wounds. They've been hit by napalm bombs, hand grenades, mortars (not all by VC, either; many are hit by mistake by friendly forces) . . . wrinkled old men and women who appear to have aged with the earth itself; younger people, old before their time—most of whom have lost at least part of their families as a result of this conflict; children and tiny babies who lose limbs or become otherwise scarred before their lives have really begun.

Let me tell you about one patient. Two weeks ago, Dr. Short (a member of the New Zealand surgical team which works at the hospital) remarked to me that they had a Montagnard girl of about 12 with whom no one could communicate. They didn't know from where she'd come or what to do with her after she'd been released. Did we know anyone who could help her? The same day I'd met a Montagnard employee, Pedro, of USAIS; and on the chance that he spoke the child's dialect, we took him to the hospital. The girl was curled up on a not-too-clean stretcher on the floor (not enough beds, even less clean linen), crying, while a nurse tried to clean her head wound. Pedro began talking to her. She stopped crying but wouldn't look up or respond to his questions. He said she came from Kontum (how he knew I'm not quite sure). He told her when we left that we would return, which we did two days later. She still didn't speak to Pedro, but he said he had heard about her from someone in another town—that both her parents had been killed by VC and she had no family. Her tribe would care for her, so Pedro said he would keep her awhile before making arrangements to get her to Kontum. We stayed with her only a few moments, then decided to go to the marketplace and buy her some food and clothes (she wore only a ragged undershirt, and the hospital hasn't enough food to feed everyone—only 75 patients out of 500). This done, we took the things to her. Two or three days later I went back to the hospital for other reasons, and she came running to greet me. I was amazed at the change in her, and at what a lovely child she really was. She tagged along with us as we made the rounds of the hospital. The doctor said she could leave, and Pedro was to get her Tuesday, the day before yesterday. He went out there but she was nowhere to be found; nor did I find her later. The doctors and nurses didn't know her whereabouts, so we are now assuming that whoever brought her must have taken her away. A simple story with no real beginning or ending; but how many of them there must be just within that hospital.

Another activity, simple again, yet rewarding, has been visiting one of the orphanages here. About a dozen of my girls have been going, and they and the 35 children who are there love it. Holding the babies, reading to the children and singing with them, taking them cookies—they so look forward to it. One of my students remarked to me the last time we went, "This is the first time I have come with you . . . I am so sad!"

Qui Nhon has again become very hot. To compensate for this

it's best to do as the Vietnamese do: just take things easy. If you're riding a bicycle, ride slowly; if you must walk, walk at a leisurely pace—you'll get there eventually and won't arrive with sweat trickling down your face (not as much, anyway). And what would we do without the beach! The South China Sea, with its shades of green and blue, fishing boats—sails raised high—in the distance, is always inviting and provides welcome, if only momentary, relief from the scorching sun. Our Australian friend, Peter Tilley, took Sharon and me, along with other friends and some of my students, by boat to a nearby island recently. As some of our members had underwater masks, we all had a look at "the world beneath"—and what a spectacle it was! Like something out of a Technicolor feature—fish of luminescent blue color, other less impressive creatures, complete with a coral reef. Such beauty, yet so close to the many unpretty sights I see in Qui Nhon. . . .

Regretfully, it has taken well over a week for this letter to come to its conclusion (it's now April 16). Much has happened since the Monday I began it: the political situation has settled down in some areas (Saigon and Qui Nhon included), seems to have worsened in others (Hue); Tan Son Nhut airport in Saigon was mortared, killing and wounding many and causing much damage (I landed in Saigon only a few hours after it happened; at the moment am still in Saigon to work on aforementioned report); General Thi announced he is behind the rebels, which has given new momentum to the political turmoil in Corps I (Hue)—it is strongly suspected that he may have been threatened with his career or even his life by Buddhist leaders who are determined not to let their movement die, as it was beginning to do. The fall of Premier Ky had been predicted, but we think he has weathered the storm and has enough force behind him to remain in power. This is a crucial time, for, should Ky be removed, there is no one—civilian or military—who would be able to assume responsible leadership. Eventually, of course, such a leader would be found; but Vietnam would suffer even more during that interim.

What the next few days bring is anyone's guess. Schools in Central Vietnam are still closed, with no word as to when they'll re-open. We will have to make this time up, however, which is why the official closing date remains uncertain. The situation is discouraging; as a well-known American said, "A nation divided against itself cannot stand." And at times, it seems this one won't. When I asked my students recently, "Why?" these are some of the responses they gave: "We were too tired of unbelievable revolution that it did not bring songs and sunshine to us." "We wanted to show our necessary and main desires." "Living in the liberty and democracy regime, the citizen can suggest the government to realize their just yearning. With this purpose the demonstration took place." "General Nguyen Cao Ky has made a big separation in Army: Nguyen Thanh Thi has been disbanded by him. I think that, in that time, I can't agree with any separation. We must fight the enemy. Vietnamese Communist are unique enemy that we must fight to the last man." Some didn't agree with the reasons for the demonstrations themselves: "I can't consider or remark on any problem I don't learn yet." "I think that ⅔ of students wanted a holiday from school."

Am I, under these, or even under "normal" circumstances, accomplishing what I had hoped to, you ask? For now, I shall say only, "I think and hope so."

As ever,

Jeanne

CAPTAIN RONALD RALPH CLARK *was a pilot with the U.S. Air Force in Vietnam from April 1970 to May 1971. He sent the following letter home to his daughter Rhonda.*

June 4, 1970

Dear Rhonda:

This isn't exactly Irish-linen, but it does the job of real stationery. At any rate, I am proud to have been invited to your graduation. However . . . other plans have been laid for my attendance at other functions on June 11, but I will be thinking of you at that time. Be proud and hold your head high, for you are a child of love.

We have "stop the war" demonstrations here, too, Rhonda. Every day hundreds of guys get out of their foxholes, hundreds more take off in helicopters and airplanes; thousands get out of bed to support the "stop the war" demonstration. That's all we're trying to do. The kids in the U.S. demonstrate to protest those killed in campus riots—how much better it would be if they would protest those two killed in the last unarmed RF-4 that was shot down, or maybe for the F-105 pilot—another *kid*—that was knocked down by ground fire. I knew all three of them. Each was worth at least one full-scale demonstration. But we don't have time to demonstrate; indeed, there are barely enough hours in the day to *really try* and "stop the war."

The situation in Cambodia is just that—a situation. During the regime of Souvanna Phouma—a pro-red king—the Viet Cong and the VN Communists were allowed sanctuary in Cambodia. Really as a place to withdraw and lick their wounds, for the U.S. was not allowed to pursue them into Cambodia. As a result of this sanctuary they built up vast stores of matériel for waging war against South VN. Cambodia was sort of a back porch whereby they could gain access to the kitchen. But with the overthrowing of Cambodia communist government came a pro-western power who could see that the only solution to a free Indo-China was ousting of communism.

This ousting involved the elimination of the sanctuaries and the matériel dumps as well as the elimination of the concentrations of Viet Cong and NVN war-making capabilities. I say it was a situation, because we allowed them to do this in the first place, and we were fully aware of their presence there. The same thing is happening in the southern reaches of North Vietnam and Laos, and unless we go back to the bombing of the North we will never stop the movement of men and supplies into the south. Maybe that sounds like war mongering, but I am sure many of us over here feel that way. And we pay taxes too.

We managed to catch the rat pack at a party the other night and got a picture of us together which I will send on as soon as I get some prints back. We party occasionally but always have a lot of fun.

Guess I'll have to go to work now, as I'm flying tonight and need to clean up some paperwork. I think of you.

JOHN SOMMER, *a volunteer with the International Voluntary Services, Inc., wrote the following letter home to his friends.*

August 1965

Hue, Vietnam

Dear Friends:

When the red, orange, and golden streaks of sunset silhouette in black the ancient turrets of the Imperial City gates, and the sampan people silently drift from the mossy canals onto the stately Perfume River, the only sound being that of oars dipping in water, then the old Vietnamese capital city of Hue is at its most magical. At this season, Hue is unquestionably the sunniest and the hottest place in Vietnam, and the sampan people traditionally anchor for the night on the river, where is to be found at least relatively refreshing air after a torpid day. Actually, Hue is not all that old, the constitution of the inner Imperial City having been begun by the Emperor Gia Long in 1804, but time and climate have worn it down so that now one sees moss-grown vestiges of ancient eras set amidst wide esplanades or within forgotten courtyards. Lotus ponds, in addition to the Citadel moats, are dotted here and there in the city and outside too in the spacious royal tombs which bear the story of the past and glory of an earlier Vietnam.

Over the lotus ponds and blissful sunset silences, however, also whirr the blades of modern helicopter war, and while Hue struggles to preserve its character, inundations of American Marines and Army men, however much controlled by their commanders, make this increasingly difficult. The majority of Hue people will resist the bad changes, but the cyclo drivers profit and so does "Joe" Nghia, whose motto is: "You haven't seen Vietnam if you haven't seen Hue . . . and you haven't seen Hue if you haven't been at JOE'S BAR."

Into this weird mélange of atmosphere and ironic situations, the youth of Hue and of Central Vietnam are growing up. The other day a young friend asked the director of the local USIS Library if he could borrow a certain philosophy book; "Well, you could," said the director in reply, "but unfortunately that's one of the books you all burned last winter in the attack on the American library!" We all smiled lamely at one another. If Vietnamese students are proud, and therefore frustrated because in their country's present situation there is little to be proud of, Hue students are even prouder. For the imperial flavor seems to have worn off them, and some are even related to the royal family. While outsiders feel that students should be kept off the streets and that their demonstrations on political questions are mere frivolity, the students earnestly believe that it is their mission to take an interest in their country's politics and to right the wrongs they see. Indeed, to a large extent they are right, for in a country such as Vietnam they represent one of the few intellectual groups capable at all of thinking on such matters. The only point which might be argued is whether they are able to improve on the injustices and imperfections which they criticize. And this is where they are now being put to the test . . .

In this part of Vietnam the main student work is with refugees, tens of thousands of whom are flooding in from more distant, and even not-so-distant, communist-terrorized areas. In a typical refugee camp, hundreds of persons are crowded into one building, with one bed for each family; Vietnamese families often number up to one dozen. Feeling that the government is not doing its part to help the refugees, the students are running a healthy program of competition to build houses, wells, sanitary facilities, etc. In a grim war situation, their work is a ray of sunshine, for it shows they do care. In a sense their social mission appears like a last act of desperation, for they admit that they are bewildered by what is happening to their country. Their political activities have been lessened partly because they are numbed to changes in government; they are tired. Ominously perhaps, some students begin to say that if the war is not soon won, any solution at all will have to be accepted, just to end it all. In their summer social-action work, in spite of all sorts of adversities, they are energetically forging ahead. But in Vietnam one does not dare to predict too far ahead.

My role in all this has been as the American support representative for the Summer Youth Program work in the first zone. . . . Part of it has meant uninspired work over budgets and other administrative details; much of it has meant getting to know the students. So when the president of the Hue Student Union invited me to join their campout at the 17th parallel on the National Day of Shame, I accepted.

The Day of Shame, on July 20th, marks the signing of the Geneva Conference in 1954 which divided Vietnam into two parts, and this year the occasion was used to announce the government's new policy (at least for propaganda purposes) of liberating the North. We were somewhat afraid that the day itself might be chosen as the moment for doing so by marching across the border, and wondered if, as Americans, we ought to be there at just that time! But official Americans felt it would not be dangerous for us to go, so two of us went, the only foreigners present among the thousands of Vietnamese.

The Ben Hai River meanders from west to east as it forms the frontier between North and South less than 100 kilometers north of Hue. Along with Hue's Perfume River, the Ben Hai is one of the few Vietnamese rivers which are blue in color. (The others are brown.) It is a narrow river and it is traversed by a fairy-tale green wooden bridge. Only a red and white barrier pole appears to prevent one from crossing. On both sides are tiers of loudspeakers blaring propaganda across to each other, and huge signs proclaiming, respectively, "Get the Americans out of the South," and "Get the Chinese out of the North." On our side a huge yellow flag with red stripes billows in the wind, and immediately across on the other side unfurls an equally large red flag with a yellow star. Except for a few guards who paced back and forth on the opposite bank, the mobs on our side were unanswered other than by the blaring loudspeakers.

Beginning like a picnic, our Day of Shame celebration took a sudden change when, just at dusk, and led by the local province chief, a horde of students rushed out onto the bridge—stopping at the halfway point. An uncanny sight, as against the yellowing sky these young "voices of freedom" chatted with the northern border guards. Intermingled with the evening variety program later on was the voice of a Student Union spokesman reminding people that this was not a picnic but a Day of Shame for Vietnam. "We should cry," he wailed! Then, building up to a dramatic peak, just before midnight of the 20th, the students took torches and formed an awesome procession in the darkness, pacing the banks of the Ben Hai and all the while fervently singing the new patriotic song, "Vietnam, Vietnam." At exactly midnight and in great emotion, they surged again onto the bridge: "Long live Vietnam," they cried, and sang, "Vietnam, Vietnam." All the while the impersonal loudspeakers from the North droned on with their propaganda. Such is the divided country.

The next morning, after an uncomfortable night on the river bank during which many students maintained a wakeful vigil to prove their patriotism, the government organized *its* ceremony. Many more thousands of people were brought in by trucks and buses from the neighboring province, and in mid-morning planes flying overhead alerted us to the arrival by car of Prime Minister Ky, General Thi, and other dignitaries. Suddenly, nearby shots broke out! We couldn't at first figure out from where, and didn't quite know what to do. Then we realized they were coming from just across the river on the northern side—shooting at the southern airplanes in warning not to dare fly over the river into the North! The planes soon took the hint, having accomplished their mission anyway of alerting us to the Prime Minister's arrival, and they swung around again. The bands played in the morning sun and heat, the dignitaries spoke, and as their words wafted across to the North, so did the droning of the personless northern propaganda waft into the South.

And so there is both a hideous war—the shrill screeching of jets over Da Nang—and there is peace—the lotus ponds of ancient Hue. We are caught up in an ambiguous and fascinating situation, where one can see and feel all the forces of a modern Western world in an old Oriental land, acting and interlacing in the minds of an entire people. We feel as though in the center of the world today, where the forces of what we call freedom fight with those of a conflicting ideology, where the underdeveloped are coming up to the threshold of greater development, where terrorism and corruption are as commonplace as the easy smile of the Vietnamese who, in spite of everything, still has a will to live.

Sincerely,
John Sommer

SERGEANT DAVID L. GLADING *served with the U.S. Army, assigned to the 2nd Battalion, 12th Infantry, 25th Infantry Division in Vietnam from August 1969 to August 1970. He was awarded the Bronze Star, Air Medal, Army Commendation Medal with V device, Vietnam Service Ribbon, Vietnam Campaign Ribbon, and several other awards, national and state, from his 19 years in the New Jersey Army National Guard, from which he retired as Master Sergeant.*

*He wrote the following letters to his then-girlfriend, Kathryn Hawkins Glading, whom he married in 1971.*

*Sergeant David Glading standing by his bunker at Fire Support Base Pershing (photo by his radio telephone operator, PFC Steve Landry, from Massachusetts)*

22 Sep 69
8:45 P.M.

Hi lover,

Well here I am writing again! But I was sitting outside smoking a cigarette, and thinking. It's a beautiful night, moon's out, stars, and no clouds, ya don't even need a flashlight. I had just finished reading the paper and found a poem, so I'm sending it along.

You know, you hear and read about all the things that go on over here, but don't really understand or believe them until you see it. I've seen old men beat woman, girls, little boy, and young men. I've seen dead and wounded, and I've seen little children cry when their fathers are taken away. Sometimes it's necessary to save lives, but other times, mostly, it's not necessary but sickening. With one hand you beat a man and with the other hand you offer him water and a cigarette. Is it right? In the manner in which I was brought up I must say it is wrong. But after you've been here, only as short a time as I have, your ideas change. Not really change but are pushed out of your conscious mind, you must say it is right or you may never return. I sit and see all these cute little kids, I love kids, but they're old for their years, they've seen a lot, more than most Americans will ever see, or ever want to see. I hope I never see half of it. I wanted to come here, yes. And I'm glad I have come because I'll never forget, nor ever want to forget what I see. No matter how bad things get for me when I get home I never want to feel sorry for myself because I'm lucky, lucky to have been born in America. I think of little Qwin and how I'd like to be able to bring her to the states with me so she could grow up and be something besides a soda girl or prostitute! The same with the little orphan girl I used to visit in Germany. I wish these kids could have the chance to grow up the way I did, to have a chance to be somebody, anybody. Not to have to be afraid to go to sleep at night for fear of the VC or of artillery shells, to go to school, to have clothes, to have toys, good food, everything. I do my job and do what I'm told. I would never kill unless I had to but if I had to I wouldn't hesitate, I've been trained for that. But I still have a conscience, and have values of right and wrong. And to beat up someone, a human, just like me, who is caught up in the middle. Most of them don't really care either way, they just want to be left alone. I feel sorry for these people and sometimes wonder if we should be here at all, but I also know if it isn't here it'll be somewhere else. So I guess it doesn't really matter. People in America are safe at home, no worries, why should they worry about the people of Vietnam, or the communists. We are a lazy country, self-centered, money-oriented, and literally don't give a shit about anything that doesn't present an immediate or direct danger to us. There will never be a Utopia, nor will there ever be Peace. Not as long as people are ignorant to the facts, the simple facts.

I sometimes think I should have been a medic, that way I feel as if I can help a little. My letters to you are my only way to get these things off my mind. I'll last over here without any trouble, I'm not worried although I'll admit to anyone that I'm scared. I sometimes wonder what God thinks about the whole situation? Someday I'll find out. But now I sound a little "antiwar" and "longhair," which I'm not. I believe in God, love my country, and love my family and my girl. But sometimes I wish that maybe there had been a world war fought on our own shores, and in our own towns. We have no idea what war is like, it's an experience you never forget. Maybe someday the world will change, but I doubt if I'll ever see it. I disagree with a lot of things, especially politics and politicians, and "hippies" and "Black power."

18 Nov 69

Kathy,

I was reading the paper and feel kinda down because of the demonstration in Washington, DC. I guess I'm proud to be an American and proud of my country. It's still number one to me, right or wrong. Although I can't agree completely with the way the war is going, I don't agree on just up and leaving because then the whole purpose, the very reason that all these men have died for, is lost. People in the states need to have an enemy invade them, have them have to see their homes burned, their fathers killed or taken away, living in a bunker with bugs and insects just to be able to live through mortar or artillery fire, having GIs come during the day and the VC come at night. No one can understand unless they have been here. The demonstrations help the enemy more than anything else. The protests are a slap in the face to most of the guys over here. They are sent here to fight and possibly die protecting America and the other free nations. Their own people through the protesting are prolonging this war longer, thus more GIs get killed. The VC want to see the U.S. get on its knees. I don't.

I went down on the road yesterday afternoon to get a few things and my two little girl friends were there. They were about 100 ft away from me and just ran all the way to me. Big smiles on their faces and just saying "Dabid" and a bunch of Vietnamese I couldn't understand. I gave them a few cans of C-rations. They picked me some berries and gave them to me to eat plus picked a bunch of flowers and put them in my hat. They like to look at the pictures in my wallet.

*The following letter was written by* WALTER ROBINSON, *a volunteer in Vietnam with the International Voluntary Services, Inc.*

November 20, 1964
Plei-Ku, Vietnam

*Thau qui ban,*

This letter has been started several times since the last when I expected to write another part on the war. But it is a subject just too big to wrap up in two parts, for it goes on seemingly unchanged. . . .

The VC recognize village control by killing off village chiefs and their successors. By the third round, the people tend to be docile. And they may not fight at night because they are tired from the fields and do not care to shoot their friends who are forced to march in front as a shield. No village is safe. For Vietnam, it is like the old Chinese punishment of slow death by slicing. (The VC are not forgetful. The other night they murdered a woman whose husband was killed a year ago for betraying them. This happened in a village only two miles from this small provincial capital where General Khanh, as 2nd Corps Commander, launched his coup to "save the nation." Yet who could save this lady?)

It is recognized that Diem's regime brought the country together. Toward later years, it was accused of losing touch with the people, particularly in regard to the Buddhists. This aspect of big city doings, an aspect not so overt to many working here, caught the eye of our government even as it propounded that all eyes be turned to the masses, most of whom lived outside the now politically windy cities. If Diem was objectionable, access of the rural areas to our attention was no less possible then than now; in fact, was easier when I came a year ago in June, since VC activity was less.

What I am trying to say is that the main problem, or hope, has been and will continue to be, barring escalation of the war, to reach the rural people, mainly because that is where most of the people are and most of the strife. It takes the patience of people of the East, something the Vietnamese have, but which we may lack. It is not easy to say this will be a solution. But, certainly, it is a worthy goal to encourage development; for, with or without fighting, it is a way to further the independence of a country.

It is ironic that we should have to give aid to encourage the people to support the government, while the VC take forcibly what they want, whether rice or men. When one sees Montagnard existing under makeshift, bamboo woven shelter barely higher than a naked toddler's head, while the houses from which they fled in the night still smolder, when they know of no reason why this was done, it can be believed that they, and the Vietnamese, would prefer just to be left alone.

Since I work on the provincial and village level (and am very "provincial" minded) I would like to point up some of the problems which make it difficult to rely on the people quickly swinging en masse to our side in return for help. In sadness, I feel it is an extension of the lack of interest in foreign aid back home, when one considers we spend 50 billion a year for the military and only a couple for economic, a lot of which is swallowed up in administrative costs. We spend 20 billion on advertising and seldom moan if a couple of that is misspent. We will make the merchants happy by spending 15 billion this Christmas (what will be spent on cards and wrapping is what is spent in a year in Vietnam), but the money invested in human welfare for the sake of our children is not considered a necessary gamble. . . .

One might well ask why the Vietnamese, with far more personnel and public services under their control, don't initiate projects on their own. They do, but far more than is realized they are entangled in their own web of problems. The roadblocks are many and downright hard to accept sometimes. Americans often believe the Vietnamese to be inept, irresponsible, and, in bitterness, to actually want to continue the war so they can continue to receive aid. For a people so cheerful and alert, they often fail to get the full respect of

Americans who, by comparison, seem dedicated to getting the war over without fooling around, taking independent action, solving problems, getting results. If the Vietnamese have any feelings for these things, they don't show it.

In fairness to the Vietnamese, who are indeed cheerful and whose cheer is a delight to me personally, their own problems must be considered. Their biggest handicap is inheritance of decades of French rule and exploitation, when nothing was put back and cheer was the only thing to live by. (France, after the last war, was in chaos, with every man for himself.) How completely different to see Malaya, which was under British rule. Here, it is said, they build a house like the French and then tear it apart to put in the plumbing.

The Vietnamese are great on paperwork and red tape. The owner of the imperial seal in China once held the key to power and it is no less true here. . . . Officials do not move without written orders from above, especially from Saigon. Unfortunately, some programs, the terms of which are quite clear to Americans, must wait on lengthy correspondence. Yet this was helpful (everything here has a contradiction), for during turnovers at the top, those below faithfully waited for direction. They survived the French and Japanese and sometimes, in sadness, I think they are prepared even if we leave.

Perhaps they fear making a mistake and losing their jobs, for there are few other choices for advancement. A Special Forces advisor gave this as a reason when he said if he is with a group of Vietnamese soldiers on their way to a certain point and meet VC 300 yards away, the leader will not attack unless he gets orders from above. By this time, the VC have left. He said the men have the guts, that he'd just like to take over a group of them to show them what they could really do. (By contradiction, the VC hold terror in abeyance.)

To Americans, this is all foolishness, if not high treason. But the Vietnamese are so disarming, so indirect, that there is very little we can say. The American military are especially chosen and are as even tempered as any group could be. With this combination, there are almost no unpleasant incidents. Still, the Vietnamese have their own problems, even if they are too gracious to tell us about them—sometimes their own lack of personnel, equipment, and experience; a tiredness of 20 years of war; fear of the countryside; the religion of Buddhism which teaches not to kill. . . .

*Than Ai,*
Walter Robertson

SERGEANT F. LEE HUDSON III, *U.S. Army, of New Jersey, wrote the following letter home to his parents, Fred and Edith Hudson, of Pine Hill, New Jersey. It was written from the small fire support base Normandy III, where sniper fire was common and food was delivered by helicopter and served by "Donut Dollies," whose friendship and laughter was appreciated by the troops.*

*Sergeant F. Lee Hudson looking at an 8" Self Propelled at Di An (photographer unknown)*

23 Oct. 67

Dear Mom and Dad,

When Christmas time comes around, I want you to take some money out of the bank and buy a five dollar present for you and Pop and all the Mahons and Gram and Grandpop. And I'll tell you again that there's nothing that I really need, just send the food like you usually do.

My name is in for a Sgt.'s position. I may have to go before a board of inquiry and answer some questions. If I make it, it'll be a while before I find out. I'll let you know what happens.

The other day we got a large chest of games. Footballs, softballs and gloves and bats, chess, and a mess of other things. So now we have some other things to keep us active.

We've been listening on the radio and reading in the paper about all the demonstrations and marches against the war. Yesterday I heard that Stuart Symington wanted to stop all the bombings and all operations and sit and see what happens. Everybody over here says that doing it would be the worst thing possible. If we keep this up, eventually we'll end up with a North and South just like Korea was.

If the Marine Base at Con Tien ever falls or even if we move out of Con Tien on our own, you'll see one big stink and a lot worse talk. For some reason, from what I've read, people back in the states have made Con Tien something out of proportion. Con Tien is a vital spot, but it's not as big a point as it's made out to be.

It would be nice to be able to come home from here early, but not at the cost of giving South Vietnam to the Reds.

Well I've rambled on long enough. Take it easy and remember what I said about Christmas.

Love,

Lee

*The following letter was written by a young soldier to a friend in Idaho, and entered into the Congressional Record by then-Senator Frank Church of that state. In the words of Senator Church, "This letter from the field presents a far different picture from that given in optimistic official reports." Appropriate deletions were made at that time to preserve the soldier's anonymity.*

Dear Chris:

Hello from Vietnam. I'm presently about [deleted] miles south of the border between North and South Vietnam in a compound near [deleted]. I'm here for a few days to recon out some bridges that we'll have to strengthen before I can hope to get our tanks and other armor over. I am newly assigned to the [deleted] Cavalry (Vietnamese) and will take over advising a troop as soon as I get some of these recon and administrative problems out of the way. The cavalry over here uses tanks and armored fully tracked scout and support vehicles. They are fast moving and kill lots of Viet Congs. I went on a couple of operations with them last week. I went out with a troop that is about [deleted], because that is the one I will take over in about four weeks. They moved and shot very well and I doubt if our own cavalry could do much better than this. However this excellent state of morale and training of these particular troops is the exception rather than the rule in the Vietnamese Army.

Chris, I've never been so disillusioned with our country as after my experiences over here for the past five months or so. For the first time I am on the scene where the news is being made and I realize that reporters for the most part do not strive to present an accurate picture of what is taking place—rather they write what will sell and make them the most as far as money and reputation. Most of the combat photos are either posed or else they are behind-the-lines training photos captioned as front-line combat photos. After having been in combat for the past few months I have a pretty good idea of what can and cannot be done. When you see a picture of a Viet

Cong coming out of a cave with hands held high—you can bet it is a posed picture. When you see a Vietnamese mother shielding its child's body from bullets, you can bet the photographer would have his [deleted] down too. What a bunch of baloney.

However, most of my disillusionment comes from the sorry [deleted] attitude of the Vietnamese people. Especially the educated leaders of this country are so rotten, dirty, no-good thieves. They are Communist-haters but all have fat bank accounts in foreign banks. They deposit every month several times their salary in these bank accounts outside the country. In this one area—where I was advisor to the [deleted] and also advisor in psychological warfare—the U.S. Government (through Vietnamese channels) was paying salaries of 338 cadres.

The cadres were supposed to be pacifying an area five villages in size. However, there were only about 50–60 cadres working in the area. So this meant a group of about three minor government officials (Vietnamese) were stealing $4,000 per month. I reported this but nothing was done. I raised so much [deleted] about it that they transferred me out to a straight combat unit. At the same time this was going on, the Vietnamese reports were very rosy and you would believe the war was almost won. They said that we distributed some four million pills and treated several thousand villagers when we had no medicine at all—it had disappeared before it reached us—more than likely sold in the big cities. They said my battalion (250 men) killed or captured 175 Viet Cong. However, I have seen only two bodies and about eight prisoners in all of our actions. Even accounting for the ones dragged away after they're dead by the Viet Cong, I think we killed only 20. However, we lost 50 of our men killed and 35 wounded and 16 captured. I personally saw and helped carry out about 25 of our own dead—but they report we lost about 12. But these false paper reports satisfy Washington. The emphasis is not on what we are accomplishing and what actual progress is being made. Rather if you put down on paper that progress is being made it is sufficient. They are living in a dream world, but I'm afraid they are fooling only themselves—and the American public: both will suffer in the long run.

I have been trying to analyze this corrupt and inefficient plan for winning the war and determine just what is the basic reason for our continuing failure here (we are failing no matter what the newspapers and the Johnson administration says). I think it boils down to this: We have committed ourselves here in Vietnam and have stated that we will stay as long as is necessary and will put into this country as much as it takes to win the war. However, the money is given to the Vietnamese Government officials to use as they see fit. Since they are spending our money and they know we will give them as much as is necessary they accept no responsibility whatsoever to ensure that the money and supplies are used for its intended purpose and efficiently. They are on the gravy train and know it and intend to stay on it. It is a paradox—the longer the war lasts, the more money they can steal. The more money they steal, the longer the war will last; if the war is won and the United States pulls out, the salaries of these officials would drop 100 times of what it is now. So why should they try to end the war? They have nothing to gain by it and plenty to lose.

The Vietnamese people themselves—the merchants, the farmers, etc.—do not appreciate what we are trying to do for them. The restaurants and shops have two prices, one for the Vietnamese and one for the American soldiers (who are dying for these people). It costs about 16 cents for a Vietnamese to buy a beer, 40 cents for a soldier. It costs 60 cents for a Vietnamese to buy a block of ice, $2.50 for a GI. A ride on a cyclo costs a Vietnamese 20 cents, the same ride for a GI $1. I could quote these prices forever. If you insist on paying the Vietnamese (lower) price they laugh at you and refuse. No matter how many shops you try the story is the same. They have you over a barrel. A GI who spends 60 days living in a foxhole full of mud like an animal cannot just refuse to pay. If he is to get any relaxation on the half day off in town his CO has given him he must pay the outrageous prices or do without. Most just grit their teeth and pay.

Another thing the Vietnamese people do is steal from the GI. I've had cigarettes snatched out of the seat next to me while driving my jeep down the street at daylight in downtown Da Nang. I once caught the man who did it. The Vietnamese policeman I took him to spoke a few words in Vietnamese to the man and turned him loose. He smiled very sweetly at me and said, "Very sorry." Yes, they are very appreciative of what we are doing for them. The other day a friend of mine, Captain [deleted], was killed in a Viet Cong ambush. With him were about 10 Vietnamese soldiers. Though [deleted] was killed, the Vietnamese soldiers who were with him managed to fight off the Viet Cong. But when his body was returned to our command post, his watch, pistol, rifle, money, etc., were gone. Another friend of mine went to pay a visit on the company and found one of our Vietnamese allies with his pistol, another his rifle, and another with the watch. It is easy to tell since the rifle is only the type carried by U.S. personnel and the pistol was a personal 1917 model German Luger. When I heard this I wanted to go and kill some of them myself. It is so damn rotten and unbelievable. So far we've only been able to get them to give back the rifle. The [deleted] Vietnamese officers are balking in returning his things.

Well, I was for five months with a Vietnamese infantry battalion and saw quite a bit of combat in our area [deleted] miles south of Da Nang. I came very close to death several times (earned Combat Infantryman's Badge and was put in for Bronze Star). I'm going to advise a cavalry troop just north of [deleted]. The past year they had three different advisors. Two were killed and this last one was wounded. Two were good friends of mine. It makes me very angry to see my friends killed and wounded here and to put my own life on the line daily when you see the Vietnamese themselves are not trying and don't give a damn for your efforts and sacrifices. I see

Vietnamese guys and their wives laughing and having a good time together. I see many young men not in the Vietnamese military. And I ask myself why I must be on the other side of the world from my wife, and I wonder why I must fight and risk death when many young Vietnamese men do not. There is no penalty for draft dodging and if a man deserts and is found by the authorities he is only scolded and returned to the Army even if it has been years. They are not so much as fined. However, we are aware of the penalty for desertion in our own Army in time of war—death.

I suppose that it might seem that I am feeling sorry for myself and using your shoulder to cry on and I suppose to a certain extent this is the case. But mostly I feel like I need to tell at least one person back there what is really happening over here. Hope I didn't make you too angry.

Right now I'm in bed with dingy fever. It is sort of like the flu, except you have amazing diarrhea and sharp pains in the muscles. I am usually sick about two or three days per month. This country is so filthy. More men are evacuated to the United States from disease than for wounds. At least it is a good way to keep slim. I've lost 45 pounds since I left [deleted] a year ago. Will have plenty of time for eating when I get back. . . .

Your friend,
[Deleted]

SERGEANT CHARLIE B. DICKEY, *U.S. Army, of Washington, wrote this letter to his wife Jamie.*

1 June 1969

Dearest Jamie,

I'm sitting in my hootch right now, it is just starting to rain, from the looks of the clouds and the wind it's gonna be a real big one.

It was really hot today, well over 100 degrees, so hot you just don't feel like moving. Sweat just rolls off of you, like being in a sauna bath. No kidding! In fact it is just like that! Even the air burns your lungs.

My Wife, one can never realize how dear freedom is until you taste the bitterness of a war meant to protect freedom. People may scorn and protest but know that we fight for all of you who wish to be free. I know now what it means to have real freedom.

My Dearest, I must close for now, be good, be safe, remember I love you.

Your Devoted Husband,
Charlie

SERGEANT MAJOR RAYMOND EBBETS *of the U.S. Army, who re-turned to Vietnam in 1973 to work for ITT-FEC, wrote the following reflection at the suggestion of his mother.*

*Sergeant-Major Raymond Ebbets*
*(photo by Steven Johnson)*

Early 1974

It's been a little over a year since peace, as it is called, has come to Vietnam. After Feb. 1973, two countries went their separate ways, Vietnam continued fighting alone, and the United States became engrossed in its own problems.

But whether one was pro or con Vietnam, Americans should not forget what they have created here, we kindled the fire for over 20 yrs. And then left to watch it smolder on.

I served with the Army in the closing days of American involvement in 1972. The situation then was bad for both North and

South. The South managed to repulse an attack by North Vietnamese tanks and troops. Likewise the North has managed to recover from the bombing by the United States.

How has South Vietnam changed since the last American troops left? I returned in Nov. of 1973 to join the fewer than 10,000 Americans who live and work here. Problems of South Vietnam have merely switched from war problems to economically oriented problems. With the pullout of the American, the economy was left in a decaying state. Prices have increased dramatically and the piastre is devalued about every three wks. In Mar. of 1972 one dollar would buy 410P, now 590P. Even though the dollar buys more P, this is of little help since the prices of commodities have spiraled upward. In Mar. of '73 gasoline was 60P a liter, by Dec. 125P, and at present 240P or a little under $2 a gallon. This in turn has caused the prices of everything to climb. Fishermen need gas for boat engines, and the highland farmers need gas for water pumps. And then the commodities must be shipped to the cities. Prices of goods are doubled by the time they reach the Saigon markets. And the everyday working Vietnamese must bear the brunt of these increases. It is hard to make ends meet, an entire family must work to earn money. A person makes $20 a month at a typical job, this was their salary last year, the year before, and probably next year. Now the government is ready to issue 5,000P and 10,000P notes, what good are they to a person who makes only 500P a day.

The government blames the bad economy on the communists, but the people may tend to doubt this in private. The only hope for South Vietnam is to develop the oil fields in the South China Sea. But that could be years away and there simply isn't time to wait.

The Capitol city of Saigon has changed little over the past couple of years. An area originally planned for 300,000 now supports over three million, making it the most densely populated city in the world. The city streets are still filled with choking exhaust fumes, but there are now street sweepers out every day collecting the garbage from the masses. Public buildings are painted every year, and city parks are well used. Four new city bus routes have recently been opened, which has helped to speed traffic up and given the people a cheap means of transportation.

The latest government idea is to clean the city of corruption. Corrupt officials have been fired, casinos raided and owners jailed. Convoys of smuggled goods have been seized on the way to Saigon. Local cowboys or hooligans are being arrested. And the drive to eradicate drug use in high schools has also been started.

But the average person is not concerned about things which will not benefit him. He just doesn't want his food bill to climb any higher. It doesn't take much to keep the people satisfied, but when they feel little is being done they can be quickly angered. Having had so may Americans in Vietnam must have had an affect on the Vietnamese. Many people have different opinions on this subject, but I guess it is what each person observed.

In Saigon, where the American effort was concentrated, the influence was seen down to every family. Everybody, regardless of wealth, has seen or met an American and every person has owned something of American origin. Whether it is a bar of soap or an expensive TV, bought in Post Exchange or on the black market, it came from the USA. Many Vietnamese would say they are not influenced by the West, but one only has to look around in a house. Many American goods can be found, and since the source of these goods has dried up, the factories in Chinese Cholon are making imitations of everything from Clorox to Pall Mall cigarettes. Even a house may be made from old uncut Pepsi cans, donated by the manufacturers because of imperfections.

Talking with my housegirl, who speaks no English, she was telling me how bad it was that Vietnamese picked up some bad habits. Smoking, drugs, public hand holding, were some examples. I asked her if she thought she had been influenced in any way, and she said no. After I mentioned the fact that she was wearing Vietnamese blue jeans, she was quiet.

But many of the people are still totally ignorant of America and its people. All they know is the United States is somewhere over there. . . .

In fact, their entire world consists of Vietnam, Cambodia, Thailand, and Laos. They are probably the only countries they could readily locate. A man I knew asked a Vietnamese girl in Vientiane where Thuy Si (Switzerland) was. Since this is a word of Chinese origin, she could only say somewhere in China.

Even now it seems that the Vietnamese are willing to do away with the American past. In 1964 the square around the Catholic Basilica was renamed after John F. Kennedy. Now a Saigon senator wants to change the name to "The Queen of Peace" Square. After the crying statue (Fatima) of Italy that recently toured Vietnam. I asked a Catholic friend of mine why they would want to change the name. He said Kennedy wasn't really worshipped, but the people sympathized with his family. Kennedy was killed 21 days after President Ngo Dinh Diem was assassinated. Basically, he said it was a political move to win back the American support Vietnam had lost.

So it would seem the Vietnamese are willing to forget the Americans and all our help. While some people here do want to forget, a greater number do remember. Many friendships were started that will remain forever.

Many young people in Saigon study English, but never have a chance to practice. And whenever I go somewhere, some person always seems anxious to talk in English. These same people also miss American TV. Shows such as *Wild Wild Wet* (West), *Sonny and Cher*, and even *Dean Martin* are still talked about. Although they may not have understood everything they heard, it gave them a chance to hear common English. What Americans call junk shows were highly appreciated over here. American TV may be one of our better ideas to develop international friendship.

The Vietnamese-American Association founded in the '50s is still teaching English. And regularly has many cultural activities. Although there are more Vietnamese than Americans, it is a primary source for cultural exchange.

One of the saddest things to come out of the war is the problems of refugees, the wounded and the orphans. The war has displaced thousands of people who have fled the fighting to live in an overcrowded refugee center or city. Late last year heavy fighting south of Da Nang together with the typhoon forced many people to flee to the Qui Nhon area. And with them they brought malaria, Dengy Fever, and other maladies that always accompany such flights.

And an already shaken economy is further weakened by vast numbers of unemployed people. Along with the refugees are the wounded soldiers and civilians, minus an arm or leg or both. They are given their discharge and sent home, only to be a burden on the family. In June 1972 when the fierce battle for Quang Tri was waging, the streets of Saigon were filled with amputees fresh from the front. Still in uniform, the only way to get into the movies for free, they wander around without much hope of a future. People just don't hire the Vet here, especially one missing a limb. Today in 1974, I see fewer amputees, where they have gone is anybody's guess. Home, begging in some alley, suicide, to the countryside, I just can't give an answer.

There are estimates by official groups that there are 50,000 orphans in Vietnam. Although most Americans seem to believe they are the product of our soldiers, this is not the case. There are 50,000 mixed children, but is estimated only about 1,000 are in orphanages. The rest are still with their mother and family. This is not to say there is no problem. Orphanages here are perhaps better off than in a lot of countries, but things could get worse. Americans are reluctant to give because of tight money in the states. But one should see an undernourished child whose mother has just "sold" it to an orphanage, and they may think different. Although selling babies is illegal, a donation to the mother is often the only way to save a baby.

Orphanages in Saigon are lucky because they generally receive supplies before they are distributed to others. Many times things simply disappear before they reach the orphanages. Where it goes, nobody knows, but some people feel they need the supplies more than some poor child.

There are many orphanages in Saigon, the biggest being Go Vap with 1,200 and the smallest having maybe 20. The only other orphanage outside of Saigon I've been to is St. Paul's in Qui Nhon. It is perhaps the best in Qui Nhon but equal to Saigon's worse. The Vietnamese government give 20P or three cents a day to feed each child, this comes out to about $11 a year. How much did you spend on lunch yesterday?

But despite all the ills of the country, Vietnamese seem willing to wait it out, although they don't know how long that may be. When one has been waiting a lifetime, a couple more years does not make much difference. In the meantime the armies of both sides continue to fight each other into the ground, depleting both of its young men. I've heard there are seven single girls to every man over 18 in Saigon.

Was the Vietnam excursion a failure or success? Depending on which side the globe you are on will determine your answer. Americans who have never been there, are perhaps the biggest "experts" on Vietnam. College students of the late '60s, I being one, were at the top of the list, followed by politicians.

As the Vietnam Tourist Bureau now advertises, "You've heard about it, Now come and see it."